Welsh
in a Year!

Welsh
in a Year!

Fast-track your learning of Welsh

JEN LLYWELYN with Howard Edwards

Argraffiad Cyntaf: 2007

⊕ Jen Llywelyn a'r Lolfa Cyf., 2007

Lluniau: Tim Arnold a'r awdur
Cynllun clawr: Y Lolfa

ISBN-10: 0 86243 968 X
ISBN-13: 978 0 86243 968 2

Argraffwyd a chyhoeddwyd yng Nghymru gan
Y Lolfa, Talybont, Ceredigion SY24 5AP.
gwefan www.ylolfa.com
e-bost ylolfa@ylolfa.com
ffôn 01970 832 304
ffacs 832 782

Contents

Diolch i:

- My Dad and Mum for their love and support. Dad's half-Welsh, and gave me a very good start in life – he told me that when we came to Cymru on holidays as children, 'We are going abroad for our holidays – to a country with its own language and its own culture.' Thanks, Dad!
- Judes and Tim – for being Judes and Tim, two of the bestest people in the world.
- Howard Edwards – for his linguistic expertise, his professionalism, and for his terrible sense of humour – without which he probably couldn't have worked with me as well as he has!
- All who have contributed in various ways to the book, not least the Learners of the Month, and those who have been supportive and egged me on.
- My Welsh tutors along the way: Howard, Val, Felicity, Ioan, and others.
- A special thank you to three people who, by their courteous insistence, 'obliged' me to learn Welsh: Enid Gruffudd, Meredydd Evans, and the late Gwynfor Evans.
- And to others who have encouraged me along the way: Graham, Gwilym, Seimon, Mared, Rhian and Rob, Glenys, the staff at Strata Matrix, Ann, Emyr, Nia, Siriol, Lynne, and Cantorion Aberystwyth!
- The team at Y Lolfa.
- Jim Wingate – for his love and support (even in the face of my pessimism about my ability to write this book), but also for his professional input, without which the book wouldn't have got finished.
- And most importantly, The Challenger, without whom the book most definitely wouldn't have even got started!

Foreword: Nia Parry

The enthusiasm, hard work and commitment of many thousands of Welsh learners, like Jen Llywelyn, never ceases to amaze me and always uplifts me. *Welsh in a Year!* is an honest and real account of Jen's journey to fluency. It's also a useful reference book with a glossary in each chapter, learning tips and suggestions about web-sites to look at, books to read, and programmes to watch, in order to support learning.

Having had the honour of working as a Welsh tutor for years, and of presenting *Welsh in a Week* and *Cariad@iaith* television programmes on S4/C for learners, I have had the pleasure of teaching and meeting many Welsh learners from different backgrounds and areas, each of whom are motivated to learn for different reasons, and each of whom go about learning in a different way, but each of them dedicated.

How wonderful and reassuring it is to read about people like Jen, who, once she moved to Wales, felt so deeply passionate about the Welsh language that she set about learning it. If only more people had her drive and determination.

Whether you're thinking about learning Welsh, or are already on the journey, this is a book everyone should read: a book every Welsh learner will empathise with, but also a book every first-language Welsh speaker should read as a step towards understanding how important it is that they are supportive to, and patient with, learners.

Wherever you are on your journey to fluency, I reiterate Jen's wise words: "When you feel like giving up – keep going!" – and *pob lwc* (good luck) to you. The main thing is – have fun, and the words will come.

Nia Parry, 2007

Introduction

About me and Welsh

Meeting Welsh

I first met Welsh when I was a kid, coming to Wales from England with my parents and my Welsh grandfather on holidays. I loved to hear the language, and to try it. I always wanted to live here and learn Welsh. I knew Wales as 'my land' when I was 4.

Moving to Wales

Then, when I was 48, my man and I moved to Wales, and I started looking for ways of learning Welsh, believing that if I did, I would automatically become part of Welsh life, and would be 'acceptable'! I believed then, and I believe now, that learning Welsh should be obligatory for everyone who comes in to the nation – but I also believe that you can't force people to learn anything. (I am, and make no apology for being, an idealist – but a realistic idealist!) I want many, many more people to become Welsh-speakers – but happy ones, not resentful ones.

Starting Welsh

I had been in Wales for 3½ years, I am ashamed to say, before I made time to start learning Welsh. Work, house-hunting and moving house took a lot of time and energy. I was, however, tuning in all the time to the language and to Welsh culture. In October 2000 I eventually enrolled for a correspondence course in Welsh, run by the University of Glamorgan (Prifysgol Morgannwg). The correspondence course gets you to hear, read, write and speak Welsh – you have to record a short tape with each unit. I'm still (2007) slogging through this course – I find it an invaluable course to run alongside the more conversational courses I've been doing. However, when I bought it, I didn't start it for months.

I also started on a beginners' Wlpan course, which was, at that time, running for four mornings a week. But there were many snags, not least the heavy time commitment, which I found I couldn't keep. I felt at the time that Wlpan was too pressurised, and didn't fit my learning style. I wasn't allowed to look at what I was saying, and that made me feel insecure. I wasn't allowed to look things up in the dictionary, and that made me feel unsatisfied. I had to say things like, 'I live in Llandeilo', which I don't. Perhaps I'm just too rebellious, but I couldn't handle it. After about 5 sessions I abandoned Wlpan. For the time being, at least!

I sort of plodded from October 2000 to August 2001, when the National Eisteddfod at Dinbych (Denbigh) changed my life. It was around that time that I realised the terrible state of our very few predominantly Welsh-language communities – those where 60% or more of the inhabitants speak Welsh – and the amount of help they need (and are not getting). I was shocked. I think it was then that I realised that it's not enough for people to learn Welsh – no matter how many of us do it. We need to do something more to help these communities. Otherwise, as 'incomers', you and I are helping to damage these communities.

Discoveries

I plucked up the courage to write to a local 'language activist' to ask questions, and received tremendously courteous and helpful answers – all in English. I was surprised and delighted. With this new-found friend, I explored my own feelings about being an incomer, and found out all kinds of things about being a Welsh-speaker in Wales. I became much more determined to learn Welsh faster. Then in July 2002 I went to the language centre at Nant Gwrtheyrn, on the Llŷn peninsula in the north of the country, for my first course, and really got going.

The Challenge

But in August 2002 came the real catalyst for the fast-tracking bit! The Challenge. (See the relevant chapter.) THAT was the beginning of my fast-tracking. And I want to share with you my progress, and my mistakes and failures, as well as my successes. I'm sure I'm not unique. I'm sure there are a lot of other people who've also done the fast-track stuff, and if that's you, perhaps you'll share your strategies and tips with me, and perhaps I'll revise this book later and include them.

Never 'too old'. Never 'too busy'.

I should say at this stage that I am in my mid-fifties – so I don't accept the 'I'm too old' excuse! – I know learners of Welsh a lot older than me, and they're doing fine. I worked from and at home, with two part-time jobs (to pay the bills), books to write, and a PhD to do, so I don't accept the 'I'm too busy' excuse, either! I worked all through my Open University degree course, and am working now. It sounds horribly self-righteous when people say, 'How do you find the time?' and I say, 'I don't find it, I make it,' but I'm afraid it's true. It's the only way.

I am more and more convinced that learning is an attitude, not an ability. I'll say more about this throughout the book.

ME, LEARNING, TEACHING, AND YOU!

Me ...

Firstly, let me say that I'm NOT a whizz-kid! I've never been that. I was certainly 'no more than mediocre' at school, and especially at maths and languages! No-one is more surprised than me with the way I've got on with my Welsh. Having said that, I have lived and worked for 13 years beside Jim Wingate, a well-known expert in the world of TEFL (Teaching of English as a Foreign Language), and he has passed on to me a lot of wisdom and knowledge, and talked about recent research about how people learn.

Learning ...

Because *teaching* should be about that – the ways people *learn*. Some people learn by repeating and reciting things, but others don't. Some people learn by sitting quietly and concentrating, but others don't. Some people learn by speaking it first and then finding out what they have just said – others don't. But too much teaching happens because the tutor has been taught how to teach, rather than being taught to discover how people learn.

Teaching ...

And unfortunately, our whole school system has been based on that sort of idea – This Is The Right Way To Teach!

And that school system failed me in the 1950s and '60s. I could have learned maths if I had been able to have some quiet Baroque music floating around, and if I'd been able to talk to fellow-pupils about it. Music in the classroom? Absolutely **NOT DONE** when I was at school! But now, it's an accepted part of learning, and particular types of music are used for particular subjects, with excellent results. (I'm primarily an Audial person – see questionnaire of learning styles, page 19.)

The school system failed Jim, the TEFL teacher-trainer I mentioned above, also in the 1950s and '60s. He didn't learn his tables, or his alphabet, because he isn't an audial person and couldn't SEE any pattern in what he was expected to learn. He still can't look things up in a phone book, because it's alphabetical! (Jim is very much a Visual person – see questionnaire of learning styles, page 19.)

The school system failed my son in the 1970s and '80s. He could have learned a lot more if he'd been able to wander around his classroom without being told to sit down and sit still. It's now recognised that some pupils – particularly boys – **NEED** to move around while learning, and that making them sit still is quite damaging to their learning. (My son is primarily a Kinesthetic person – see questionnaire of learning styles, page 19.)

How you learn

So it's good to know that people are doing a lot of research now into How People Learn (rather than just, How Teachers Ought to Teach, which has hitherto been the case). I will be building a lot of this research into this book. Thing is, if you know how you learn, you can learn efficiently and quickly – even if you are not altogether happy with your tutor's style. Have a look now at the questionnaire of learning styles on page 19. Do the questionnaire and find your learning style. Then read the book, but be thinking about how you learn, and what you have found helpful and unhelpful in your learning career so far.

Your messages from school

It also will help to remember, and perhaps discount, the messages you received when you were at school. These messages might be positive and helpful ones, which have stayed with you all your life so far. They might, though, be unhelpful negative messages – which have also stayed with you all your life so far. (My main school message was, 'You're never going to be any more than mediocre in anything you do, so don't aim for anything more or you'll be disappointed.') Trouble is, if you get these messages at the 'right' age, and you perhaps aren't as confident as you could be, you tend to believe the messages! I certainly did! People have NO RIGHT to decide when you are a child what you are going to be like throughout your life! I think it's meant to make us 'buck our ideas up', but it doesn't work for most people. In fact it has the opposite effect.

Your messages to yourself

For a while, during my 40s, I went from 'You're always going to be mediocre' to the other extreme of 'I'm going to be The Best', but that was too much like hard work! Now, I want to be the best I can be at everything, but I'm not 'driven'. If other people think I'm 'mediocre', then that's OK with me. I choose how I feel about myself, how fast I work, and at what point I stop thrashing myself to improve.

Your own ways of learning

Knowing how I learn helped me a lot when doing my first degree with OU – the Open University (I graduated in 2001, at the age of 52). OU is hard work (though I'd recommend it to anyone), but as an Audial person, I know that if I put quiet slow music on when I'm reading, I read better (a CD with songs on it is unhelpful because I sing along and lose concentration, and anything too emotional is too distracting, because although I'm not Kinesthetic physically, I am emotionally!). If I talk things through with someone, I can clear blockages much quicker. If I write something, it improves enormously if I read it aloud to myself and can hear where I haven't expressed myself clearly.

Your own incentives and motivation

I say again, I'm more and more convinced that learning is an attitude, not an ability. And particularly, *learning Welsh* is an attitude. Some people say, 'You don't *have* to learn Welsh.' But to live in Wales and choose *not* to learn Welsh is to refuse to speak to many people here in their own language! (And I could add: so why, then, should they speak to *you* in *yours*?) But even for *starting* to learn, you need some kind of personal incentive.

It isn't enough to say, 'I'm learning Welsh because I feel I should.' That's not a strong enough motivation, and you're going to give up when things get tough, or when other things are more important.

It isn't enough to say, 'I'm learning Welsh because I live here,' or, '… to prove to the Welsh Nationalists that I support their language.' It's better, and will probably mean you learn the language eventually, but it's going to take you a long time.

What about, 'I'm determined to learn Welsh well enough to be able to enjoy the Eisteddfod without translation equipment, to watch S4C without the subtitles, to read Welsh books and newspapers, to have reasonably natural conversations with my neighbours, and to enjoy the wonderful wealth of culture that is waiting for me when I cross the bridge into Welsh life'?

Your own target

Give yourself a target. And 'Because I WANT TO!' is the best one.

We WILL be pleased you're learning Welsh, but YOU need your own 'internal motivator', as academics call it! – which is, your own nice tasty carrot, or, if you don't like carrots (like I don't), your own huge bar of chocolate, or bowl of ice-cream, to keep you focused when things go wrong, or when you feel tired or stupid, or all those things at once.

I wanted to do my degree quickly, and I did – in five years, which isn't the quickest possible, but pretty fast. My 'large bar of chocolate' was that I wanted to get my degree and all that knowledge into my head, and have its benefit for the rest of my life. The downside of this was that I rushed through courses, lurching from one assignment to another, and I feel I missed out on a lot of the information in those wonderful books.

Learning Welsh fast isn't like that. OU is past and gone. Welsh is with me every day. OU was finite – learning Welsh is a lifetime's experience. Every day I learn more. Every time I start feeling 'Learning Welsh is too hard for me', another wonderful Something happens, and I know I will never stop, never give up. The experience of learning Welsh is nothing compared with the experience of Wales itself, and the literature, music, culture, and thinking that is the heartbeat of the nation. The faster you learn the language, the quicker all this will be within your reach!

Your fellow-learners

Here are six characters who have enrolled for a series of Welsh workshops. They are all on Welsh-language classes once or twice a week, but these once-monthly workshops (the first one residential, the others a full morning) will give them some more depth and more chance to talk about Welsh, and the process of learning Welsh, as well as some revision and some new material. They are typical of the people I have met on courses. It's the sort of mix of people you're likely to meet on your first course (like I did on mine). Perhaps you can see yourself in there somewhere! The problems they have will, likely, be the problems you meet. And the conversations they will have in their sessions are the sorts of conversations I have had, and heard – and you might hear! – about people's anxieties, their ideas about Wales and Welsh, and their discoveries along the way about Welsh, and about learning Welsh.

Mike, in his 20s. Incomer to Wales. Works in public sector in Gwynedd. Learning Welsh for work, but has no real interest in Wales or in Welsh. Red-head with stereotypical temper! Enjoys walking, fishing, and DIY.

Dafydd, in his 60s, from Caerdydd. Now retired. Had Welsh-speaking Mam-gu and Tad-cu (grandparents – southern version), but his parents spoke English. Therefore he remembers odd phrases from his childhood. Wife, Helen, English, wants to learn but hasn't started yet. Likes his garden, but also into politics, and quite fiery. Is passionate about the Welsh language.

Rob (50s) and **Sally** (40s). Living near Machynlleth. Rob is a potter, Sally an artist and herbalist. Their children are in a Welsh-medium school, so they have decided to learn, largely to help the kids with their homework. They feel they 'should' learn, but have no emotional commitment. Very 'green' and eco.

Anka, in her 20s, from Ljubljana in Slovenia. She is learning Welsh because she loves languages generally, and Welsh in particular – and loves Wales, too. She speaks German, French and Italian already. Is studying Medieval Welsh in the University, but speaking modern Welsh is quite a new experience. Anka's mother is learning English.

Marian, retired school teacher, in her 50s. Geraint, Welsh-speaking northern farmer, married her 6 months ago – on condition she learns Welsh! Loves jazz and reading. Geraint keeps Welsh Black cattle, and he and Marian train sheepdogs.

Your tutor: Howard Edwards

Howard is in his 50s, married, with two kids. He lives in the north of Wales. Howard learned Welsh as an adult, and then trained to be a tutor. At school, he wasn't good at languages – they turned him off! But when Howard decided to learn Welsh, his first tutor's sense of humour meant that the classes were fun! (More about Howard on page 158.)

This book

You have met me. You have met your fellow learners. You have met Howard. Now meet this book, and find out how it works.

- If you're a Visual learner, you like to see the overview of a book first.
- If you're an Audial learner, you want to hear this book speak to you.
- If you're a Kinesthetic learner, you're probably impatient to turn the page and get on with it, but you do like to know how a book works!

If you turn to p. 19, you will find a questionnaire to help you find out whether you are Visual, Audial or Kinesthetic – or a combination of any of these. You will understand the book better after doing this questionnaire, but more importantly, it will help you with learning Welsh – learning any subject, come to that – and also, how to get on with your fellow-learners, your tutor, and even with members of your family!

Framework of a Unit

Each unit is a month – starting with July – relating to my own 'year' of learning Welsh.

- My own experience: my problems and crises, solutions and victories. I hope you will find that helpful.

- Book of the Month

- Various learning tips, suggested websites, language tips and other items to help and interest you

- The Welsh Workshop – a monthly 'get-together' for the six Welsh language learners featured in the book. These workshops are informal sessions in which the tutor introduces everyday grammar and vocabulary, with exercises you can do, and the learners share problems and solutions. They also have conversations about Welsh and the process of learning. I hope these conversations answer some questions you have never liked to ask – and will raise other questions too. Let me know! (And perhaps another book will evolve from your comments!) You can use the Glossary at the end of each month, and the Word List at the end of the book, to understand the Welsh in the workshops, and to write your own answers. It's worth it!

- Learner of the month: hear about someone else who has learned Welsh and uses it in everyday life, to prove that it's possible!

How do you learn best? Tick the boxes then turn the page for an explanation.

A	B	C
I learn by listening, by talking to others, and by talking to myself. I try out things by talking them through before doing them.	I learn by seeing. I need an overall view and purpose. I am cautious until I'm mentally clear.	I learn by doing. I like 'hands on' experience. I do it first, then talk about it or see it being done.
I'm talkative and may monopolise the conversation. I tell the whole of an event in sequence.	I need the whole picture and lots of detail. I select carefully what to say. I communicate vision and pictures.	I'm not very talkative. I use gestures and movements. I use action words. I communicate feelings.
I enjoy reading aloud and listening. I'm confident with unknown words.	I'm a strong, successful, fast, quiet reader. I prefer to read than be read to.	I enjoy action-packed books and stories with a strong plot. I reflect the story with body movements while reading.
I'm easily distracted. I can repeat things accurately. I can mimic accents, tone, pitch and timbre. I speak rhythmically.	I'm neat, orderly, quiet, observant and organised. Appearance is important.	I move a lot. I respond to physical rewards, e.g. touching rather than words.
I remember words or what I hear. I memorise by repeating words in my head.	I remember what I see. I memorise by picturing. I have problems remembering spoken instructions.	I remember an overall impression of what I experience. I memorise by doing.
I'm better at talking than writing. I like to talk to others or myself while writing.	I have naturally neat handwriting. I like my writing to look good. I'm quiet, careful and deliberate.	My writing is thick, pressured and unclear. I'm a physical, emotional writer.
I spell words as they sound (phonetically), not as they look. I spell rhythmically.	An accurate speller. I see the words. I'm confused about spelling unfamiliar words.	I count out letters with body movements, e.g. moving my finger. I check my spelling with my internal feelings.
I hear sounds and voices. I'm good at sequences and creating dialogue. I'm responsive to music.	I see vivid images. I can see possibilities, details appear. I'm good at long-term planning and at overviews.	I want to walk while imagining. I like to act out the image. I'm weak on details, strong on actions and emotions.

If you ticked most in column A, you are a predominantly Audial learner.

If you ticked most in column B, you are a predominantly Visual learner.

If you ticked most in column C, you are a predominantly Kinesthetic learner.

Many tutors and teachers teach mostly to the Audial learners. If you are Visual or Kinesthetic, you may be disadvantaged. But by understanding your learning preferences, you can take responsibility for your own learning.

Tips for Audial Learners

During lessons: say and repeat the new words and pieces of grammar aloud (or whisper in your head), practise in pairs, imagine saying the new words in a dialogue, ask questions.

Between lessons: say the new words and pieces of grammar again in different ways, sing them, chant them, create new dialogues, imagine saying the new words and pieces of grammar in situations.

Tips for Visual Learners

During lessons: write and draw the new words and pieces of grammar in a mind-map or in word families, picture the meanings, use colours on your notes, write titles and subtitles for each topic.

Between lessons: rewrite your notes more completely and neatly and colourfully; look back at previous notes and rewrite, redraw or recolour them, every five lessons make summary diagrams.

Tips for Kinesthetic Learners

During lessons: do actions (or imagine doing them) for each new word and piece of grammar, associate feelings and emotions with each new word and piece of new grammar, draw action diagrams with the words and pieces of new grammar, act out dialogues and texts (or imagine doing so).

Between lessons: move around, gesturing, while saying the words and pieces of new grammar, and acting them, create practical situations using the words, collect words into groups to do with feelings, e.g. words you love/hate.

Getting Ready

So now ... Here are the six learners, getting ready to leave for the Welsh workshop. They are all attending classes once or twice a week, but they feel the monthly workshops will give them a bit more concentrated information, and help their progress.

Mike:	Hello, Brian. Thanks for looking after the house for me while I'm away. Hmm ... Now, where is that tin of maggots? If I get bored over the weekend I'm going fishing.
Brian	Hi, Mike. That's a good idea. You won't like being stuck in a classroom all day. Especially learning Welsh. I don't understand why you are going to learn Welsh.
Mike:	Nor me. I'm learning because of my job, not because I want to. I don't see the point. Everyone in Wales speaks English anyway.
Brian:	It's a waste of time. What does it do for you?
Mike:	Me? It gives me a chance to go fishing and get paid for it!

Helen:	You are lucky, Dafydd, going on this workshop. I wish I was.
Dafydd:	Yes, darling, but someone has to look after the garden! Someone has to take the dog for walks!
Helen:	I suppose so.
Dafydd:	I'll talk to you in nothing but Welsh when I get home, then you'll learn quickly.

Helen:	Or feel stupid.
Dafydd:	No, really, it's the best way. Nothing but Welsh.
Helen:	Oh dear ... Dafydd?
Dafydd:	Yes, dear?
Helen:	Why are you packing that book?
Dafydd:	What book?
Helen:	*Car ... Carn ... Carnifal.*
Dafydd:	It's a political novel in Welsh. And by the time I finish the year I intend to have read it!
Helen:	Oh dear ... I can see I'm going to have to get my Welsh dictionary out while you're away!

Sally:	Now, Mum, remember to sell my pictures if anyone comes to see them.
Rob:	And my pots.
Mum:	They all have prices on them, I see. Thank you. That makes it easier! But tell me again why you are learning Welsh. I don't understand.
Sally:	Well, we live here.
Rob:	We have Welsh friends. The kids have lots of Welsh friends, don't you, Grace?
Mum:	But they speak English!
Rob:	They can, but...
Grace:	Gran, I've got some Welsh friends who can't speak much English!
Mum:	Don't tell fibs, Grace.
Grace:	No, really, Gran. They have grown up in families that speak Welsh, and all their friends speak Welsh, and they only heard English on the telly a bit. Now, they are learning English in the school playground, when we play with them, but they still speak mostly Welsh. They don't like speaking English. And that helps *us* learning Welsh!
Mum:	But it's most important to speak English!
Sally:	Well, Mum, perhaps to you it is. But to them, and many people we know, it's more important to keep Welsh alive.
Rob:	Which is another reason for learning it. You ready, Sal?
Sally:	Bye, Mum! Bye, Grace. Give Anna and Jonny a kiss from me when they get home from Anwen's party!

Anka: [on phone] Hello, Mum! Lovely to hear your voice! How's Ljubljana? Hot? ... I can imagine it, full of tourists, nowhere to walk, all the squares and bars full! Horrible! ... Yes, I'm talking in English. Why? Because it will help you with your English! Me? I'm getting ready for a workshop. ... Yes, I know I'm always doing courses and things! ... This one? It's a Welsh workshop. ... No, not medieval Welsh this time, this is modern Welsh. ... The difference? I suppose it's that this is the Welsh that people speak every day, in pubs and offices and on the street. ... In Ljubljana? Mum, it's not going to do me any good in Ljubljana! I'm not coming back there to live! I tell you every time we speak! ... I'm coming back to see you in September, for a fortnight, then I'm coming back to Wales.

Marian: Geraint – whatever is going to happen to Jess when I'm on the workshop?

Geraint: Happen to her?

Marian: She is going to forget her training.

Geraint: She won't forget, you'll see. Dogs don't forget.

Marian: I am a bit worried about *my* training!

Geraint: About what?

Marian: That you expect me to come home speaking faultless Welsh.

Geraint: No, really, it's there to improve your Welsh, not to turn you out at degree level! There's only two things I want you to learn at first.

Marian: And that is ...?

Geraint: I want you to tell me you love me, in Welsh.

Marian: [laughs] I expect I can find that out from someone! What's the other thing?

Geraint: 'Geraint! Your tea's on the table!'

Marian: Get away! You think that's all a woman's useful for!

Geraint: [laughs] 'Na ti! [There you are!]

July / *Gorffennaf*

The first month of my story

I drove to Nant Gwrtheyrn on a wet afternoon at the beginning of July. I felt very nervous. Twelve days is a long time to be stuck with lots of unknown people, in a tiny village halfway down a cliff! That alone was daunting – but the reason for being there was even more so. A Welsh course for beginners. I'd done little bits of Welsh, but was afraid the others would be better than me.

It's difficult to define 'beginners'. I would say the only 'total beginners' in Welsh are people who have just moved into Wales, never even having been here on holiday. If you live in Wales, you see Welsh everywhere. All children in state schools learn Welsh. Public sector information is, by law, in Welsh as well as in English. Road signs and place names give you a lot of Welsh. So everyone who lives here, or has holidayed here, has seen Welsh – and most likely used it, too, if only asking in a fumbling and shy way for directions to somewhere! You know it is a spoken language (and therefore, a language possible to learn) because you also hear it in most areas, and on television and radio. But where do you go from there, if you want to improve your Welsh?

I hoped 'the Nant' would tell me! I'd heard it was a good place to learn. I checked in, and took up residence in one of the Nant's cottages. Spartan, but adequate. I was self-catering, so I didn't meet anyone that night. After a breakfast-time walk down to the sea and back the next morning, and with substantial butterflies, I followed the crowd up to the teaching room. Fifteen other people. Very assorted ages, types, motivations, and abilities.

Howard the tutor arrived, and immediately I knew it would be all right. He is warm, kind, funny, and learned Welsh himself as an adult. That means he really understands the things we find puzzling. He instinctively suits the Visual, Audial, and Kinesthetic learners.

This is not to say, of course, that the Cymry Cymraeg (native Welsh-speakers) can't teach Welsh! There are advantages to both. But maybe for beginners a learner of Welsh is better? (Tell me what you think!)

Anyway, off we went with the weather … so far, in my experience, all courses start with the weather! This seems odd, but truly, this is the first topic of conversation when Welsh people meet, and it's a good 'sounding board' for finding out how people are feeling! (And of course, here in Wales, the weather is just a little important.)

Howard's lessons were great – revise a bit of the previous lesson's grammar etc, introduce some new stuff, do various activities that get you using what you've learned, lots of laughter. During the fortnight, we learned all the basics of Welsh, and with Howard's encouragement, we quite quickly got into speaking Welsh with each other at break times and in the evenings, as much as we could.

We also discovered something of the culture of Wales – cynghanedd (the strict metre poetry that is uniquely Welsh); penillion (a form of accompanied singing that is, again, unique); information about the ancient pilgrimages of saints along the Llŷn to Aberdaron and thence to Ynys Enlli; and we enjoyed a voyage to the island itself.

The fortnight at the Nant did my Welsh a power of good. At the end of the first week I was exhausted. At the end of the second, I drove home feeling as high as a kite, thrilled with the knowledge that I could learn the language. I found myself thinking in Welsh – obviously not deep philosophical thinking, but thinking nonetheless! I felt Howard had given me a wonderful start with the language, and I was ready for the next step.

When I got home I immediately found out about courses for adults in Aberystwyth, my nearest town. I had two choices – either I could get onto one of the four-week summer courses in the town, or I could wait for the end of September, when the new classes started. I decided to wait. My fast-tracking hadn't yet begun!

Book of the month

The Welsh Learner's Dictionary **Heini Gruffudd (Y Lolfa, £6.95)**

A dictionary. There are many, but this is the first one I recommend. It is helpful for beginners in that mutations are signposted, so it's easier to look words up, plural forms are given (which is very useful indeed in that there are at least 13 ways to make plurals in Welsh!), and there are some very useful bits of grammar explanation in the front.

Learning tip

Learn to pace yourself. Learn when to walk away from books, go and look at the sea, have a bath, do the washing up, whatever. Your brain will be still be processing stuff even if you think you've forgotten Welsh. **It's no good fast-tracking if you wreck yourself in the process!**

July: Sesiwn Fawr

– a weekend of Welsh music of every kind in Dolgellau. Rock, pop and folk, and probably also what I refer to as 'Country and Welsh'.

 ## Website of the month

www.s4c.co.uk/cymraeg

There are a lot of good websites for people learning Welsh. One of the fun ones is the one from S4C, the Welsh-language television channel – or, should I say, the terrestrial channel which has the most Welsh-language programmes. This website has lots of information, and a very useful pack of materials – a tape, a booklet, *All You Need to Know About Learning Welsh, But Were Too Afraid to Ask,* giving loads of information about courses; booklists, a badge, and a lot of other information and encouragement! If you don't have internet access, you can order the pack by phoning the Welsh for Adults Information Line, 0871 230 0017.

• Language tip of the month

WORK ON PRONUNCIATION FROM THE START! Everything depends on it! Be prepared to feel silly, but do it, get it right, and you will find everything is easier, and what's more, people will understand you!

The Welsh Alphabet

The Welsh alphabet is different from the English one. For a start, there are 26 letters in the English alphabet, but 28 in the Welsh one. Here it is:

a	b	c	ch	d	dd	e	f	ff	g
ng	h	i	l	ll	m	n	o	p	ph
r	rh	s	t	th	u	w	y		

Welsh doesn't have j (except in borrowed words like garej and sosej), k, q, v, x or z.

There are seven vowels: a e i o u w y (remembering that w and y are vowels will help a lot with pronunciation).

The so-called 'double letters' – ch, dd, ff, ng, ll, ph, rh and th – are technically called 'digraphs', and count as one letter, including in true Welsh-language crosswords and in the newly available Welsh-language Scrabble.

Welsh Workshop

Mike: Hello! Are you looking for Howard Edwards' group?

Anka: Yes. It's here somewhere. I hate these buildings. All the rooms look the same.

Mike: We'll know our way soon. You're not from here, are you?

Anka: No, from Slovenia.

Mike: Oh! Why the … Why are you learning Welsh, then?

Anka: This is the room! No-one's here yet. Why? Because it's a beautiful language.

Mike: Is it? Oh!

Anka: Why are you learning?

Mike: Because I have to, for work. No other reason. Ah, here's someone else.

Dafydd: Hello! I've just met Howard and he's on his way.

Anka: Is he nice?

Dafydd: Boi neis iawn.

Mike: Sorry?

Dafydd: Seems all right to me. I'm going to sit here, I'm a bit deaf. Someone else coming?

Sally: Are we in the right place for Howard's workshop?

Mike: Hope so!

Rob: There's someone else coming – Marian. Is that all of us, then? Only six? I wanted there to be more people so I could hide!

Anka: I wanted about this size of group, that's nice. We'll get lots of attention!

Mike: That's what I'm worried about …

Howard: Ah! Helo! Bore da!

All: Bore da!

Howard: They told me this is a beginners' workshop, but you all speak Welsh already!

Marian: Well, bore da is pretty standard. And diolch, and nos da. And iawn, of course!

Howard:	Wrth gwrs! Da iawn. Océ. Wel, Howard dw i. I am Howard. Howard dw i. Dw i … Howard dw i. What is your name? Beth yw'ch enw chi?

Howard: Wrth gwrs! Da iawn. Océ. Wel, Howard dw i. I am Howard. Howard dw i. Dw i … Howard dw i. What is your name? Beth yw'ch enw chi?
Anka: Oh! Anka … dw i.
Howard: Da iawn, Anka! Diolch. A chi? Who are you? Pwy dych chi?
Sally: Er … Sally dw i.

Your turn!

Beth yw'ch enw chi? (What is your name?)	
Pwy dych chi? (Who are you?	

Sally: Howard, may I ask a question, please?
Howard: Of course! That's what I'm here for! I may not be able to answer it, of course, but it's worth a try!
Sally: Well, I just wondered. In English, we don't say, 'Who are you?' It's rude. So why isn't it rude to say it in Welsh?
Howard: Ah – a good question, and an important one. In Welsh, a lot depends on the intonation, on the way you say things. So, if you say 'Pwy dych CHI?' as if you're interrogating, then it can be rude, yes. But if you say it gently, with a smile, with the emphasis perhaps more on the 'dych', then it is perfectly acceptable and normal. Does that answer your question?
Sally: Yes, thank you!
Howard: The same applies in a lot of Welsh questions and so on. You can ask and say quite direct things, in a gentle and courteous way, and it doesn't come out rude. It's quite a useful skill to carry over into English! Now then, moving on: Ble dych chi'n byw? Where do you live? I live in Llandudno Junction. Dw i'n byw yn Llandudno Junction. Dw i'n byw – I live. Marian, ble dych chi'n byw?
Marian: Ooh, er, dw i'n byw yn Rhosgadfan.
Dafydd Dw i'n byw yn Penrhyncoch.

Your turn!

Ble dych chi'n byw? (Where do you live?)	

Howard: I'm from Abergavenny originally. Y Fenni = Abergavenny. 'Yn wreiddiol' = originally. Dw i o'r Fenni yn wreiddiol.
Anka: Dw i o Slofenia yn wreiddiol.
Mike: Dw i o Wrecsam yn wreiddiol.

Your turn!

O ble dych chi'n dod yn wreiddiol? (literally: from where do you come originally?)	

Howard: Tiwtor dw i.
Mike: Oh, right. Jobs. Pensaer dw i. I looked that up in the dictionary.
Rob: Artist dw i.
Sally: That's cheating, Rob. Croch ... croch ...
Rob: Old croch?
Howard: *[laughing]* Crochenydd?
Sally. Probably. Crochenydd dw i. Diolch, Howard.
Anka: Stiwdant dw i – ? Is there a Welsh word for 'student'?
Howard: There is – myfyriwr, or myfyrwraig because you're a woman. But there's a lot of political correctness creeping into Welsh now, and we'll look at the 'wraig' stuff a bit later. Myfyriwr is OK for now. Dafydd? Beth dych chi'n wneud? What do you do?
Dafydd: Well, I've retired, so I'm doing nothing!
Howard: Dych chi wedi ymddeol. Marian?
Marian: I'm what they call 'just a housewife', I'm afraid.
Howard: Gwraig-tŷ! But you're a farmer's wife, I'm sure you're not 'dim ond gwraig-tŷ!'
Marian: Too right I'm not! What's Welsh for overworked dogsbody?

Your turn!

Beth dych chi'n wneud? (What do you do?) (OR, what are you doing?)	

Howard: Oce. Rŵan 'ta. What have we said so far? Let's recap. Get into pairs and ask and answer about your name, where you live, where you are from originally, and what is your job.

Your turn!

Pwy dych chi? (Who are you?)	
Ble dych chi'n byw? (literally, Where are you living? Where do you live?)	
O ble dych chi'n dod yn wreiddiol? (Where do you come from originally?)	
Beth dych chi'n wneud? (What do you do? – and also, What are you doing?)	

Howard: That's fantastic! You're having a conversation – saying true things about yourself in Welsh, and asking questions! Well done! Now we'll go on to look at some other things, some of the components that make up a Welsh sentence.

Sally: There's something called a 'verb-noun', isn't there?

Rob: Very impressive, Sal, but you don't know what a 'verb-noun' is!

Sally: Thank you, Rob, and neither do you! I was going to ask …

Howard: Right. In Welsh, a verb-noun is a word that can behave as a verb or as

a noun – they are mostly used as verbs in Welsh sentences but are also used as nouns. They can be used like the '—ing" form in English. For example: Dw i means I am. So we couple this to the 'verb' with a small word, yn as follows. Take darllen = to read , for example. We have:

I am	in the state/process of	reading

This conveys: I am reading. It can mean I am reading here and now as I speak or I read as in I read the paper every morning before going to work. The yn is abbreviated if it comes after a vowel, so we have: Dw i'n darllen – I'm reading / I read.

Anka: Oh, I thought the yn conveys the ing bit, and I'm obviously wrong.

Howard: Yes, quite a number of people think that, Anka, you're not alone there! Here are some other examples:

Eistedd	to sit	**Dw i**	**'n**	**eistedd**	I sit/I'm sitting
Byw	to live	**Dw i**	**'n**	**byw**	I live/I'm living
Meddwl	to think	**Dw i**	**'n**	**meddwl**	I think/I'm thinking
Hoffi	to like	**Dw i**	**'n**	**hoffi**	I like

Rob: Unfortunately, Howard, I don't like grammar!

Howard: You don't have to like grammar. It's something you can pick up as you go along, without realising it – like children do, if you think about it, when they are learning their mother tongue. There's certainly no need to worry about it. Right now, I'm going to give you the full present tense table of Bod – to be. Here it is:

Dw	i	I am
Rwyt	ti	You are
Mae	o	He is
Mae	hi	She is/it is
Mae	Idris/Siân	Idris/Siân is
Mae	Idris a Siân	Idris and Siân are (still using *mae*)
Mae'r	plant	The children are (still using *mae*) (NB: *y plant*, but y goes to 'r after a vowel)
Dyn	ni	we are
Dych	chi	you are
Maen	nhw	they are

Note that we use the same form for Idris and Siân as we do for just Idris. Or indeed just Siân! Now, if I give you ten new verb-nouns, you can make loads more sentences. With just one pattern you can make a thousand sentences!

Anka: A thousand?

Howard: You can count them as we go along if you like! I'm sure we'll get somewhere near it!

Mike: That sounds too good to be true. It can't be that easy.

Howard: OK, let's get cracking. Here are some more examples of statements:

Dw i	'n	gweithio	I'm working.
Mae Idris	yn	cysgu.	Idris is sleeping.
Maen nhw	'n	chwarae.	They are playing.
Mae'r plant	yn	bwyta.	The children are eating.
Dan ni	'n	hoffi siocled.	We like chocolate.
Mae Idris a Siân	yn	caru Cymru.	Idris and Siân love Wales.
Dych chi	'n	yfed gwin drud.	You are drinking expensive wine.
Mae e	'n	mynd i Aberystwyth.	He is going to Aberystwyth.
Mae hi	'n	bwrw glaw.	It is raining.
Mae hi	'n	coginio.	She's cooking.
Dw i	'n	gweld Siân heno.	I'm seeing Siân tonight.

Howard: OK, now make …

Anka: … seventy new sentences! Great!

Howard: Well, you've got time to write about six before coffee time!

Marian: Howard, I need some verb-nouns about cows and sheepdogs!

Howard: I don't know much about cows – grass in one end and milk out the other and that's your lot. See if you can find the following verbs in a Welsh dictionary: to – milk, chew, bark, growl, run, low (mooo), lie down, stand.

Your turn! Write six sentences!

Coffee time

Marian: Howard, I'm really worried about mutations.

Howard: Don't worry, Marian. There are so-called 'rules' that describe mutations, but it's nothing to get worked up about. Just be aware that 'Croeso i Gymru' changes where 'Cymru' becomes 'Gymru', for example.

Mike: They change the spellings just to make it difficult!

Howard: A mutation is primarily a change in the sound at the beginning of a word in the spoken form. 'Spelling' is the wrong way of looking at it. The letters are what you see written on paper. They reflect the change in the primary medium of language which is the sound of the word in speech. It helps you, Mike, to pronounce it clearly.

Anka: All Celtic languages have systems of mutations.

Howard: Right, Anka. There are different types of mutation. How a word is mutated can depend on where it is in a sentence or what word (or type of word) immediately precedes the word in question.

Dafydd: Do we have to learn all the mutations now?

Howard: People will understand you perfectly if you never mutate when you speak Welsh, although it can sound a bit odd to the seasoned speaker. I have heard one or two politicians, who have learned Welsh, speaking the language quite fluently, but without many of the mutations. OK, it is noticeable, but they are still able to express themselves very well in the language. Think of becoming proficient in mutations as an acquisition process which occurs over a period of time.

Mike: English is much more sensible!

Howard: Well, is it, Mike. Mutations happen in English, but English doesn't help with writing it as it's pronounced. I've heard Cockney people say things like: 'I've got wum brother' ('one brother'). Here the sound n becomes an m before a b. Similarly, in Welsh: ym Mangor (in Bangor). Here, the yn = in and pronounced 'unn' becomes an ym (pronounced 'umm') before the B in Bangor. Scan a Welsh newspaper to see more examples of odd-looking spellings of place names – like 'ym Mharis', for instance!
Another example in English is where people would say 'ingcome tax' instead of 'income tax'. Here the n becomes an ng before the c. This is very similar to 'yn Cymru' becoming 'yng Nghymru'. This doesn't look very nice on paper – it actually sounds like 'unghumree'. These two examples are called nasal mutations, because when you say n, m or ng, you breathe the air out through your nose!

American English is interesting. 'Twenty' becomes 'twenny'. The n gobbles up the t. The t is nasalised. 'I'm going to take a vacation' becomes 'I'm gonna take a vacation'. So you see, Mike, it's not just Welsh!

Mae'r plant yn eistedd yn yr ardd.

Learner of the month: Lari Parc

'I have no Welsh connections at all – in fact my father was English and my mother was from Austria. I fell in love with Welsh when I was about 15. Later, I was hitch-hiking, and a driver taught me 'Diolch yn fawr' for 'thank you', and 'Os gwelwch yn dda' for 'please', but when I asked him to tell me what 'yes' and 'no' are in Welsh, he just rolled his eyes to the sky!

'He told me, 'We are in Arfon, and that is an afon' – pointing to the river. And I could hear the difference between 'Arfon' and 'afon' because of his rolled 'r'. A woman told me, 'That's the Afon Dyfi, spelt d-y-f-i, not d-o-v-e-y, like the English spell it.'

'I began to learn Welsh in England, when I was 30 – I could get Welsh radio in the west of England – and I began to develop a real interest in the fate of the language. In 1987 I bought petrol in Welsh for the first time, and felt very pleased with myself! I moved to Wales in 1992, and fell in love with the place, as well as with the language.

'It took me another three years to bring my Welsh up to A-Level standard. I didn't have any major snags with the language itself, just my own anxiety that I would never learn it well. I have a learning disability called Dyspraxia, too, which makes learning anything into a slow process. But the fact that I'd managed to learn enough German to communicate fairly well helped enormously. I'd done that – not in school, but by myself – and so I could do the same with Welsh.

'I put my progress down to several things:

• Being prepared to make a fool of myself.

• Realising that in Welsh, as in other languages, being able to ask a question in the new language, but not understand the answer, is a normal part of the process.

• Being stubborn and refusing to give up.

• Learning things by heart – and putting this into my everyday routine.

'My advice to learners is: 'When you feel like giving up – CARRY ON!'

Lari taking part in a language protest – on a tower of Castell Caernarfon!

Glossary

nant	stream	gwraig tŷ	housewife
Gwrtheyrn	Vortigern (King)	wedi ymddeol	retired
Cymry Cymraeg	Welsh-speakers	gwin	wine
Cymru	Wales	drud	expensive
cynghanedd	form of Welsh poetry	i	to
penillion	form of Welsh song	croeso	welcome
sesiwn	session	siocled	chocolate
Ynys Enlli	Bardsey Island	heno	tonight
mawr (fawr)	big	hoffi	to like
gweithdy	workshop	gweithio	to work
mis Gorffennaf	July	cysgu	to sleep
bore da	good morning	bwyta	to eat
nos da	good night	caru	to love
da iawn	very good	bwrw glaw	to rain
da	good	gweld	to see
wrth gwrs	of course	yfed	to drink
beth	what	mynd	to go
pwy	who	coginio	to cook
yn wreiddiol	originally	gwneud	to do
o	from	dod	to come
tiwtor	tutor	byw	to live
pensaer	architect	eistedd	to sit
crochenydd	potter	darllen	to read
myfyriwr	student	meddwl	to think

August / Awst

August 2002 was a long month, waiting for my next course to start. However, in the meantime I decided to learn what I could about the Welsh-speaking life. I started with the National Eisteddfod, held that year at Tyddewi (St David's) in Sir Benfro (Pembrokeshire). Two Welsh-speaking friends offered to take me there and tell me about it, and what it means for the Cymry Cymraeg (Welsh speaking Welsh people).

The Eisteddfod is very special. Some people call it 'A whole nation in a field'. Many people find it a tedious week of networking and gossip. Many more (including me) enjoy it. Learners who've reached some kind of proficiency love it because it's how Wales should be – the first language of communication is Welsh, not English. Everything on the stages in the various Pavilions is in Welsh. There is Welsh song, dance, drama, poetry. There is the Gorsedd of the Bards (congregation of prominent people, dressed for ceremonies), and the Archdruid.

By the time I got on to the Maes (the Eisteddfod field is always called 'the Maes' – sounds like 'mice'), it was raining and the aisles between the stands were 6' deep in mud. I met Dylan and Nia and we had coffee. Nia was going to compete in a folk-song competition, and went off for her 'Prelims'. Dylan and I wandered around the stalls and he pointed out (in English, bless him) various aspects of Welsh life to me – things I would have missed without his help. He told me, for instance, about the Pabell Lên – the Literary Pavilion – and about the Talwrn y Beirdd, which is a poetry competition in which people have 20 minutes to write a poem of a particular type, on a particular topic (or with a given first line or last line), and then read it from the stage. The adjudicator is as much part of the experience as the competitors!

It was a wonderful 'world', that Eisteddfod day. Welsh all around me. Northern Welsh, Southern Welsh. Academic Welsh, and old farmer types winning literary prizes. Very little English around. Another huge incentive to learn Welsh.

When Dylan and Nia and their family were in the Pabell Lên (waiting for one of their sons to read a poem which had won a prize), someone else went up to be awarded a prize, and I recognised her as Alison Leyland, whom I had met at the Sioe Fawr (the Big Show), Llanelwedd (Builth), in 2000. The year before, Alison had won the Learner of the Year award at the Eisteddfod. I talked with her at the show (feeling very inadequate beside someone who had learned Welsh so well), and she had encouraged me to start learning. It was great to see her get a literary prize at Tyddewi, particularly because one of my ambitions is to write in Welsh – I'd thought it would be impossible for a learner, but obviously I was wrong!

By 2pm I was frozen and soaked. The wind was shaking the whole Pavilion. People with stalls were fastening them down to stop books, leaflets and other things being totally ruined. I decided to go home.

I'd used a lot of English that day, but I'd also learned a lot about being a Welsh-speaker. I'd also learned how small the 'family' is – there is a saying, 'Mae pawb yn nabod pawb yng Nghymru' – 'Everyone knows everyone in Wales'. It seemed to be true. Everyone seemed to be everyone's second cousin, or second cousin's second cousin! It made me all the more aware that you have to be careful what you say and do in Wales! It pays to be courteous here.

The Eisteddfod made me even more determined to learn Welsh. Perhaps I could 'do an Alison' and write something in Welsh! Suddenly the chasm between me and the Welsh-speakers seemed less daunting. Everyone I'd met had been so nice and so welcoming, and so pleased that I'd started learning.

I did another couple of units of the correspondence course during August, and started receiving emails in Welsh, and making some sense of them with my dictionary at my elbow. Tedious, but incredibly useful. I tried reading books and magazines, but found it too difficult. I knew that to have learned

Welsh would be the most wonderful thing in the world for me, but learning it seemed like a huge struggle.

Then came the end of August, and the catalyst for my fast-tracking. A Cymro Cymraeg (Welsh-speaking man) friend asked me what my policy was for my Welsh learning. 'Oh, I'm definitely going to carry on with it,' I answered.

'But what is your five-year plan for Welsh?' he persisted.

Now, I'm a typical Piscean. I have no idea what I'm doing this evening, let alone tomorrow or in five years' time, and even if I make a plan, it will probably change! His question took me by surprise. 'What do you think it should be?' I stalled.

'Right. Well, for a start, what if we plan to have a meal together, all in Welsh, on 1 September next year?'

Ha ha, I thought. 1 September 2003? No way! Too much pressure. And what if I fail? I asked him, 'What if I don't manage it?' And he just smiled. I could have hit him.

I felt completely beaten, inadequate, and very unhappy. The schooltime message came back to me: 'You'll never be any more than mediocre, so don't expect anything more from yourself.'

But if I didn't do it, I couldn't face my good friend, ever again! What WAS I going to do?

• Tip of the month

A challenge can feel to some people (for example, pessimists like me!) like a huge mountain. It is worth the struggle when you get to the top, but on the way up it can feel as if you've made a really bad mistake by accepting the challenge. Remember – there are people to read about in this book who have learned Welsh, and now use it all the time, all day and every day. You can do it too!

Book of the month

The University of Wales Press has published a really good series of Pocket Guides to various aspects of Welsh life and culture. One of them is *The Welsh Language,* by Janet Davies, who herself learned Welsh as an adult. It's very readable, and for a small book, it's extremely full of facts and information about the history of the language, right up to the current situation. Highly recommended!

A Dilemma

'But isn't Welsh a difficult language to learn?' I've heard this so many times – and from the Cymry Cymraeg, as well as from learners!

I decided early on that Welsh couldn't be a difficult language to learn in itself, because tiny children speak it, incomer children learn it really quickly, and many adults have learned it. I also realised that it is, however, difficult to learn Welsh – in Wales! There is no reason to 'struggle' with it, as we might have to with, say, German in Germany (it's clear to me that 'struggling' makes for progress), and no reason why you HAVE to use it every day. It's so easy to give up. It's so easy to see a road sign in Welsh and English, and 'see' the Welsh, but 'read' the English. There's too much English around. And also, alas, too many Welsh-speakers switch to English – even when a learner has started a conversation in Welsh!

What can we do, then – those of us who really want to learn Welsh? Well, ignore any pessimists, for a start! And when you reach the stage when you can use some Welsh, use it. And if you have bizarre conversations (like I've had) when you are using Welsh and the Welsh-speaker is using English – KEEP USING WELSH! At least you are practising, and the other person's responses will tell you if your Welsh is understandable. Their attitude is a challenge, and it doesn't help us learn, true, but it's up to us to carry on! In time, they will realise a) you are serious about learning their language, and b) that you are able to make some sort of conversation. Remember, they are not necessarily unsupportive of us learners, they just don't quite now how best to help us, and most of the Cymry Cymraeg are extremely supportive of – and joyful about – people who want to become competent in Welsh.

A brief history of the Eisteddfod

The National Eisteddfod is held every year, alternately somewhere in the north and somewhere in the south. The first recorded bardic competition was held in Cardigan Castle in 1176, but it is in 1789 that the present Eisteddfod has its roots – and in London, oddly enough! A group of North Walians, living in London, developed the Eisteddfod, while a fascinating and complex man, Iolo Morganwg, established a group of poets and musicians called 'The Gorsedd of the Bards of the Island of Britain', which in 1819 (in Carmarthen) became part of the Eisteddfod.

And so now we have the Bards, the Archdruid, lots of poetry and music, all on one field, for a whole week in August. Everything on the stages is in Welsh – no English is allowed on the stages at all – and at the moment everything on the field is in Welsh, more or less.

However, go to an Eisteddfod! You will be welcome. There is translation equipment available; there are people to help you. And remember, this is what Wales should be like! – the language everywhere. Plenty for learners to see and hear! (And buy! – books, CDs, and lovely things – jewellery, clothes, and all sorts.) And there is a place specially for us learners – Maes D – the learners' own pavilion, where there are lots of events taking place throughout the week. And of course, there is the Learner of the Year competition!

 ## Website of the month

www.llgc.org.uk/lp/lp0263.htm

This is a bibliography for Welsh learners, set up a few years ago from the huge catalogue of books in the National Library of Wales (Llyfrgell Genedlaethol Cymru – the llgc in the website address). You could either read these books in the Library itself, or borrow them from a lending library, or try to buy them through bookshops (please try to use small bookshops where possible), or (failing all else) Amazon.

If they are out of print, there are many second-hand bookshops – such as Siop y Morfa, in Rhyl, which has got me lots of out-of-print books, and I'm sure they would be pleased to do the same for you.

Welsh Workshop

Sally: Hello, everyone! Lovely to see you again. Phew, it's hot! Did you go to the Eisteddfod?

Marian: I went with Geraint for about four days. It was baking in the caravan!

Rob: I read somewhere that there are more caravans per head in Wales than anywhere else in Europe!

Marian: Yes, I'm sure that's because of the Eisteddfod. There are acres of caravans! But ooh, it was hot. I hardly slept a wink. But I enjoyed it.

Dafydd: I went for one day. I enjoyed it too, but I'm sure it will be better when we understand more Welsh. It's a huge incentive to learn!

Howard: Bore da! Bore braf! Lovely day! How are you all?

Marian: I've got lots of questions for you!

Howard: Ooh, dear, I feel suddenly faint!

Sally: Yes, I've got questions too!

Dafydd: I've got a problem with questions too, Howard! I've got the statements, I can talk about myself, but I'm so slow making questions!

Anka: [laughs] I can make the questions, but I can't answer them!

Howard: Right – I want to do more work on closed questions, and then you'll be getting somewhere.

Mike: Huh! I stand more chance of getting somewhere if I go fishing!

Howard: No, really, you just need more practice. Do you understand the principle of 'closed questions'?

Rob: Er, no, not really, no. Can you give me a clue?

Marian: I'm glad you said that! Thanks, Rob!

Howard: Right, then. A closed question is one that has a 'yes' or 'no' answer, like 'Do you like pizza?', unlike an open question, like 'What food do you like?' But in Welsh, we don't simply say 'yes' or 'no' to this type of question!

Rob: Oh dear. I wish I hadn't asked now.

Howard: Hmm. Yes, I see that my answer hasn't really helped at all! Well, here really is a clue! Are any of you old enough to remember that television game show 'Take Your Pick', where they had the 'Yes-No Interlude'?

Marian: Erm – I think that's a closed question! Yes, unfortunately I am!

Dafydd: I hate to say it, but yes, me too!

Anka: I have a distinct disadvantage here, since I was living in Slovenia at the time!

Mike: And I'm only twenty-five!

Sally: Oh, yeah! And I'm twenty-five, then! But certainly, too young to remember that.

Howard: Right. Well, it was a game where the contestants had to answer a series of questions without saying 'yes' or 'no' in the answers. So, here are some questions – do NOT say 'yes' or 'no'! Dafydd, can you play the piano?

Dafydd: N ... oh! ... er ... I can't.

Howard: Mike, is it raining?

Mike: It's not.

Howard: Sally, do you like ice cream?

Sally: Yes! Oh, no, I'm out.

Howard: Rob, does Sally like ice cream?

Rob: Er ... she does.

Howard: Marian, are sheepdogs intelligent?

Marian: They are!

Howard: Anka, do you love Ljubljana?

Anka: Yes, but I love Wales better – oops! I said 'yes'!

Howard: You see how you need to listen carefully to the question before coming out with the answer. If you go to the Irish Republic, you'll hear people answer like this: 'Is there a bank nearby?' 'There is'. The same principle. Are you with me so far?

All: We are!

Howard: Well done! Right. Look at this table. The principle is here. Don't worry too much, though: you can't be expected to learn all this in one go!

Statements	Questions	Answers	
		Positive	Negative
Dw i'n darllen nofel.	**Ydw i'n darllen nofel?**	**Ydw.**	**Nag ydw.**
I'm reading a novel.	Am I reading a novel?	I am.	I'm not.
Rwyt ti'n byw yn Abertawe.	**Wyt ti'n byw yn Abertawe?**	**Ydw.**	**Nag ydw.**

You live in Swansea.	Do you live in Swansea?	I do.	I don't.
Mae Idris yn hoffi coffi.	**Ydy Idris yn hoffi coffi?**	**Ydy.**	**Nag ydy.**
Idris likes coffee.	Does Idris like coffee?	He does.	He doesn't.
Mae Idris a Siân yn cysgu.	**Ydy Idris a Siân yn cysgu?**	**Ydyn.**	**Nag ydyn.**
Idris and Siân are sleeping	Are Idris and Siân sleeping?	They are.	They aren't.
Maen nhw'n chwarae.	**Ydyn nhw'n chwarae?**	**Ydyn**	**Nag ydyn.**
They are playing.	Are they playing?	They are.	They aren't.
Dan ni'n mynd i'r dafarn.	**Ydan ni'n mynd i'r dafarn?**	**Ydyn**	**Nag ydyn.**
We are going to the pub	Are we going to the pub?	We are.	We aren't.
Mae Gwilym yn caru Sioned.	**Ydy Gwilym yn caru Sioned?**	**Ydy.**	**Nag ydy.**
Gwilym loves Sioned.	Does Gwilym love Sioned?	He does.	He doesn't.
Mae hi'n bwrw glaw.	**Ydy hi'n bwrw glaw?**	**Ydy.**	**Nag ydy.**
It is raining.	Is it raining?	It is.	It isn't
Dw i'n coginio.	**Dych chi'n coginio?**	**Ydw.**	**Nag ydw.**
I'm cooking.	Are you cooking?	I am.	I'm not.
Mae'r plant yn chwarae criced.	**Ydy'r plant yn chwarae criced?**	**Ydyn.**	**Nag ydyn.**
The children are playing cricket.	Are the children playing cricket	They are.	They aren't.

Note that there are slight variations between dialects: North – dan ni, ydan, Nag ydan, South – dyn ni, ydyn, nag ydyn. So some Welsh-speakers say 'nac' and others say 'nag'.

The sentences and answers given are written out in full – first-language Welsh-speakers speak what I would call 'Turbo Welsh', and things are abbreviated just as things are in English:

> A: Where's the bus ?
> B: Sgon. (It has gone.)

The first example in this table is given for completeness. We don't usually go around asking ourselves questions, then answering them! Exactly the same nciple as above is applied to asking and answering closed questions in all the other possible tenses. So we construct a similar table with:

Would they like a holiday in the Bahamas ?   They would./They wouldn't.

Ydy Idris yn mynd i'r dafarn? Is Idris going to the pub?	**Nag ydy. Mae e'n mynd i'r clwb rygbi.** He isn't. He's going to the rugby club.
Ydy hi'n braf rŵan? Is it fine now?	**Ydy, wir.** It is indeed.

Howard: As it happens, I've compiled a list of questions and a list of answers. Here they are. See if you can match an appropriate answer to each question. The answer can be either a positive one or a negative one and you don't necessarily need to know every word in each question to come up with an appropriate answer. There might well be more than one possible answer for each question. Draw a line to the right answer(s).

Your turn!		**Answers**
A	**Dych chi'n hoffi Jaffa Cêcs?**	Ydyn
B	**Ydy Idris yn mynd i'r Capel?**	Nag ydyn

C	**Wyt ti'n gweithio heddiw?**	Ydyn
D	**Ydyn nhw'n cysgu?**	Ydyn
E	**Ydy'r plant yn yr ysgol heddiw?**	Nag ydy
F	**Dych chi'n yfed gwin coch?**	Ydw
G	**Ydy hi'n bwrw glaw?**	Nag ydy
H	**Ydan ni'n mynd allan heddiw?**	Nag ydw
I	**Ydy Idris a Siân yn byw yn Llandudno?**	Ydw
J	**Ydy hi'n darllen?**	Ydy

Howard: Don't forget that these responses can be used to agree or disagree with statements that people make. Try the following – This'll help you with your arguing and debating skills in Welsh !

Your turn!

Mae'r plant yn chwarae criced.	Agree	.
Mae Idris yn gweithio heddiw.	Disagree	
Maen nhw'n cysgu.	Agree	
Dan ni'n gweithio dydd Sul.	Disagree	
Mae Idris a Siân yn priodi dydd Sadwrn nesa'.	Disagree	
Mae o'n naw deg oed. (90 years old)	Agree	
Dw i'n lwcus iawn.	Agree	
Mae Cymraeg Mrs Williams yn ardderchog.	Disagree	
Mae'r siec yn y post!	Disagree	

Coffee time

Marian: Howard, I felt a bit overwhelmed. We all met up in a café on the way here. I spoke Welsh, but I didn't understand the answers.

Howard: That's normal, Marian. Don't let it get to you. The Welsh speakers who answered have had a lot more practice than you!

Rob: They certainly have! Years of it!

Howard: Persevere, and you're bound to get there. Remember they're doing you a favour by continuing to speak Welsh.

Mike: I did! I persevered!

Sally: He did! Mike just kept saying, 'Yn arafach, os gwelwch yn dda', and they spoke slower!

Howard: You will understand more and more as time goes on. Tell me what you can do to hear as much language as you can.

Marian: My husband's family speak Welsh. I could listen to them more.

Sally: You don't ignore them, do you?

Marian: [laughs] No, but I do tend to tune out.

Howard: You have tuned out in the past. Try tuning in from now on.

Rob: Radio is good, and TV.

Anka: No good in Slovenia! [laughs]

Dafydd: I can send you my tapes and CDs when I've finished with them. That'll help me move on.

Howard: Yes, listen actively with tapes and CDs but also passively with the radio. You need to get used to Welsh sounds, including the ones that don't exist in English, typically the ll and the ch.

Anka: I think learning any new language feels like you're spinning a lot of plates at once.

Howard: Yes, you are dealing with a lot of things – sounds, words, word order in sentences – both in listen/speak mode and in read/write mode. Listening is very important. Your brain will be taking things in without

your realising. It's natural to listen quite a lot before even starting to speak. Some say it's essential, and I agree. But there's no 'perfect' way of learning a language. We all learn in different ways. Discover the way that suits you – but every learner of any language should do lots of listening!

Marian: I do lots of listening to my Welsh tapes – I go into a dream! I washed up the same bowl three times the other day!

Howard: Listening is crucial to pronunciation, and pronunciation is crucial to your progress with Welsh. If you get that right, you will know how to spell what you hear, and therefore where to look it up in the dictionary. It's not like 'bough', 'enough', 'through', 'cough' in English – all 'ough' words but pronounced differently. Welsh is consistent.

Mike: Another way it's better than English. Oh – er – *easier* than English, I meant.

Dafydd: And we'll sound more Welsh if we can *say* it properly!

Ydy Twmi yn cysgu? Nag ydy, mae e'n meddwl am fwyta!

Learner of the Month: Christine James

I was amazed during the Eisteddfod 2005 to find that a learner of Welsh had won one of the major competitions: the free verse. I didn't think it was possible for learners to win the big prizes! Christine's success inspired me, and I asked her to contribute to this book in the hope that her story will inspire you too!

'People often say that learning a language is like crossing a bridge; the metaphor is a good one, but an even better one is that of climbing a mountain, since it emphasises the sweat and tears which are so often involved! Climbing a mountain – physical or metaphorical – demands time and effort. Some sections of the climb will be easier than others: sometimes the climber will be tempted to give up, convinced that the summit is beyond reach. But eventually – with persistence – the mountain can be conquered. And what a view there is from the top!

'Learning any language opens a whole new world for you, one which, perhaps, you never realised was there. You will be enthralled by things you never knew existed before starting out on your linguistic climb. For languages are keys to cultures, to ideas, to literatures; they are windows on world-views, on people and their psyches. What better reason can there be for starting to climb – and sticking it out to the top!

'I started climbing my linguistic mountain many years ago, in a grammar school which urged the more academically-minded pupils to study French and Latin rather than Welsh and Cookery, during a period when learning our national language was generally considered to be a waste of time. Resisting pressure to 'do French' with the rest of my academic peers was one of the first slopes which I was forced to tackle – and there were plenty more to come! But if progress at school was sometimes painful, nothing could have prepared me for the culture-shock of finding myself in a Welsh-language hall of residence at university in Aberystwyth. That was my personal rock-face, when I thought, during my first term, that I'd never make it.

'Yet now I cannot begin to imagine what my life would be like had I not learned Welsh. I would almost certainly not have met my husband, nor, therefore, would I be the mother to our three children. I would certainly not be in my present job – teaching Welsh literature at Swansea University. And I would most definitely not have won the Crown at this year's National Eisteddfod for writing a series of poems in Welsh.

'So have I reached the top? Does winning the Eisteddfod Crown mean I have reached the summit as regards learning Welsh? Scarcely! Languages are organic, constantly shifting and changing, and there is always something new to be learned, something more to be mastered. For me, part of the adventure of climbing any linguistic mountain is that there is always, just a little further ahead, another summit to conquer, another peak to climb. Native-speakers and learners alike, we are all still climbing. We are all still learning. And that is where the metaphor proves inadequate. The thrill of languages, unlike mountains, is that there really is no 'top'.

Glossary

sir	county	nofel	novel
maes	field	coffi	coffee
pabell	tent	rŵan/nawr	now
llên	literature	criced	cricket
bardd/beirdd	bard/bards	heddi(w)	today
sioe	show	ysgol	school (and also ladder!)
pawb	everyone	coch	red
Morgannwg	Glamorgan	allan	out
Gorsedd	throne	dydd	day
llyfrgell	library	dydd Sul	Sunday
genedlaethol	national	dydd Sadwrn	Saturday
morfa	marsh	priodi	to marry
tafarn	pub	caru	to love
braf	fine	siec	cheque
nesa(f)	next	araf/yn araf/yn arafach	slow/slowly/slower
naw deg	ninety	adnabod/nabod	to know (people, places)
oed	old	gwybod	to know (things)
os gwelwch yn dda	please (formal/plural)	chwarae	to play
ardderchog	excellent	bwrw glaw	to rain

September/*Medi*

Over the next few days I thought of very little other than The Challenge: to speak nothing but Welsh at a supper date in a year's time. Half of me wanted to take it up – the competitive half of me – and the other half, the more everyday half, said, 'Don't be daft, it's too much pressure, you can't do it.' I thought back to other things I've tried, and failed at, and I knew I couldn't do it. But then, there were other things I'd tried, and succeeded at...

And I didn't want to be sitting in Welsh classes for years and years! I wanted to be getting on with Welsh literature and poetry, and really being able to enjoy the Eisteddfod, and being able to help more usefully with campaigns for human rights in Wales.

I remembered the place I'd first been really aware of Welsh, and I decided to go back and have a look. I drove down through Ceredigion and turned right to Cei Bach. I'd been there when I was 8, in 1957. I remembered the lovely old farmhouse, the warm hospitality, and the farm workers and the shearers calling to each other in Welsh, and Mrs Lewis and her husband talking quietly in the evenings, Welsh hymns on the radio on Sundays, and the language floating around me.

But when I got there, the old farmhouse was standing miserably empty and neglected in a sea of caravans. The Welsh language had disappeared.

This is happening all over Wales, of course, but because of my happy memories of that wonderful holiday, it suddenly became very personal for me.

And suddenly the decision was made. It was almost as though I hadn't made it myself, it was made for me. YES! I will do it, I will learn Welsh – to the highest standard possible, and in the shortest time possible, because then maybe I can help the language survive in the areas where it is currently strongest, and perhaps some of the strongly Welsh-language communities will survive.

My attitude to learning Welsh completely changed. I felt very impatient throughout September. I really wanted to get on with my learning, but it would be weeks until term began!

I switched on S4C on Sunday evenings and sang the Welsh hymns. I watched things like Pobol y Cwm, the Welsh-language soap. During the week you can get the subtitles by bringing up page 888 on Teletext, if you have it. On Sundays the subtitles come up automatically. It's a good exercise, if you're disciplined enough, to watch during the week with no subtitles, and check out on Sundays how much you've understood!

The Prifysgol Morgannwg correspondence course took up quite a bit of my time.

The month seemed endless, but at last it was time for the Monday morning Wlpan session for beginners (I'd signed on for Year 1, Monday and Wednesday mornings). It was a big class, with a lovely gentle tutor. Val was herself a learner of Welsh. I found the Wlpan course this time far less pressurised than I had those years before.

The Wlpan course I started is divided into 72 units, including some revision sessions. Each unit takes 2 hours. The general idea is to get people to talk, to use the language. There is a bit of written homework sometimes. Some tutors let you look at the course book – I was fortunate, Val did, which fits in with my learning style. Others don't, preferring to get you to listen to, and use, Welsh, before looking at it. There are lots of activities which are fun, and fun is a good way to learn a language! (Or anything else, come to that!)

Because of the Nant course, I was already familiar with quite a lot of Welsh phrases, and had used them with friends outside classes. So for me it was comfortable in Val's class, and I began to relax. Until coffee break! Val came over to me.

'You know a lot!' she said. I expressed surprise – it didn't feel that way to me! 'Are you sure you're in the right class?'

'Er – um – what do you suggest?'

'How about going up to Year 2 – Tuesdays and Thursdays?' Val asked.

'Oh! Um – are you quite serious?'

'Perfectly serious!' said Val.

I'd found her style very relaxing, and I didn't really want to leave her for another tutor. 'Who will the tutor be?'

'Me!' she laughed – and I felt reassured! She obviously felt I could do it, even if I didn't. So home I went – very worried that I would be out of my depth, but it suited my 'as fast as possible' policy.

• Tip of the month

Decide to be prepared to get out of your 'comfort zone'. If you want to fast-track, don't do a year's class and then do that class again the next year to make sure you've got hold of everything. Move up! Tell the tutor you want to fast-track. Expect to feel out of your depth from time to time, but keep swimming! There's lots of us already in the water – you won't drown!

TV programme of the month

Well, although I wouldn't normally recommend a TV soap, I will for *Pobol y Cwm!* Not necessarily for the storylines (though you might get hooked, of course!), but for the language. With S4C, a lot of programmes have subtitles on Teletext, and you can choose between the English ones on 888, or the simplified Welsh ones on 889. I prefer the former. You will hear people say things and see the translation, and think, 'Oh, I could use that!' or, 'Oh, that's how they say …' It's quite 'south Welsh', but don't let that put you off if you live in the north – you might need to talk with us Hwntws (southerners) one day!

Website of the month

www.bbc.co.uk/wales/learnwelsh

Lots of stuff on this site! Including a list of grammar points. Worth trawling around to see what you can see.

Book of the month

Another in the University of Wales Press's series of Pocket Guides is one for *The Place-Names of Wales.* Hywel Wyn Owen has put together a list – not an exhaustive list – of place names, from which you can assemble most of the place names you will come across. You will also see that places with names we take for granted as 'Welsh' – like Mold – have real Welsh names! Other books in this series are about Welsh literature, customs and traditions, history, and quotations. The books cost around £4.99.

Owain Glyndŵr

On 16 September 1400, Owain Glyndŵr, from the north of the country, proclaimed himself Prince of Wales. Glyndŵr was a remarkable man. He was one of the nobility in Wales, and had studied law in London for a time, and his home at Sycharth was quite a cultural centre. But Glyndŵr was very aware of the plight of his people, and the need for Wales to be independent of England's oppression. By 1405 he ruled Wales, and had made plans to make the Welsh church independent of Canterbury. He made fair laws and established a Parliament. He wanted to establish a Welsh university too – sadly, that didn't happen until the late nineteenth century.

But by 1413, after a series of battles, the English had beaten Glyndŵr. The battles were hard-fought – even though the scene of one of Glyndŵr's victories, the hill beside the church at Pilleth (near Knighton), where many of the fallen of both sides are buried under three huge pine trees, is one of the most tangibly melancholy places I have experienced.

Glyndŵr may well have been Wales' last chance for independence. But many say he didn't die, and will return when we need him most …

Welsh Workshop

Marian: How are you doing, Sally? Personally, I am really pleased. I am understanding much more of my relatives' Welsh now. Geraint is delighted. How about you and your children?

Sally: Yes, it's lovely, I can talk to my kids' friends in Welsh a bit now, and their mums, but Rob still goes a bit blank.

Howard: Bore da, bawb!

All: Bore da, Howard!

Howard: Sut dych chi bore 'ma?

Rob: Oh. Stuck already.

Anka: I think it's, da iawn, diolch.

Mike: Oooh, hark at her! Teacher's pet.

Anka: Yes, well, Mike, I live in Wales, and I listen to Welsh whenever I can.

Mike: Well, I live here too, and I know bore da, and diolch, so I'm not too bad.

Anka: And just how long have you lived here?

Mike: Only ten months.

Anka: Ten months? And that's all you know?

Howard: Now, now, you two.

Anka: It's a matter of manners as much as anything.

Sally: Oops. We lived here for ten years before we got round to learning. And now we're realising how much we've missed by not learning earlier. So Mike's better off than us.

Howard: I'm with Sally there. In any country you can learn such a lot about that country and its culture by learning the language. It's not just a case of learning words. And now you're all learning fast. So let's get on with it! Today I want to tackle another tense. I told you last time that 'yn' is the equivalent of 'in the state of' or 'in the process of'. Remember? So each of you, give me a sentence with 'yn' in it (which often shortens to 'n, like in 'Dw i'n mynd'), and I'll write your sentences on the board.

Sally: Dw i'n darllen ... er ... what? ... um ... oh, nofel. Dw i'n darllen nofel.

Howard: Da iawn, Sally. Nesa?

Rob: Oh ... er ... Dw i'n hoffi pasta.

Dafydd: Dw i'n hoffi politics. What's politics in Welsh, Howard? I need that word!

Howard:	Gwleidyddiaeth, Dafydd. Nesa!
Anka:	Dw i'n mynd i'r Alban.
Marian:	Dw i'n … oh, dunno the word! – enjoio – coginio.
Mike:	You enjoy what?
Marian:	Cooking. But I don't think that's the correct word for 'enjoy'.
Howard:	Well, to tell you the truth, a lot of Welsh-speakers use 'enjoio'! But there is a Welsh word, mwynhau, and I will be teaching you the Welsh words for things. Whether you choose to use the Welsh words or the Wenglish words is up to you. What about your sentence, Mike?
Mike:	Dw i'n mwynhau pysgota!
Howard:	Good. Now then, we have these sentences on the board. Can you think how we could change them to the tense which conveys: 'I have done' something?

yn/'n
Dw i'n darllen papur newydd.
Dw i'n hoffi pasta.
Dw i'n hoffi gwleidyddiaeth.
Dw i'n mynd i'r Alban.
Dw i'n mwynhau coginio.
Dw i'n mwynhau pysgota.

Anka:	I've heard 'wedi' a lot – is that it?
Howard:	'Wedi' it is! So, what would we change, then?
Dafydd:	Well, if 'yn' is 'in the state of', surely we wouldn't need that?
Howard:	Right! Da iawn! So, Sally, give me your 'have' sentence. In Welsh and in English.
Sally:	Dw i … er … wedi darllen nofel -? I have read a novel.
Howard:	Right! And the rest of you, I want you to come up to the board and write in your sentence. In Welsh only.

mis

3

yn/'n	wedi
Dw i'n darllen papur newydd.	
Dw i'n bwyta pasta.	
Dw i'n astudio gwleidyddiaeth.	
Dw i'n mynd i'r Alban.	
Dw i'n ysgrifennu llyfr.	
Dw i'n plannu tatws.	

	Iawn! Da iawn. Dych chi WEDI ysgrifennu [gestures writing] ar y bwrdd? – diolch yn fawr!
Mike:	Dw i wedi ysgrifennu ar y bwrdd … er … hefyd.
Howard:	Da iawn, Mike! Unrhywun arall?
Sally:	Dw i wedi darllen papur newydd, Yr Independent.
Rob:	Dw i wedi bwyta pasta.
Howard:	Just a small tip – 'bwyta' is often pronounced 'bita'.
Rob:	So, I'm a bit stuck – how do I say 'I have eaten', if bwyta is 'to eat'?
Howard:	Well, that's where Welsh gets good. Whereas in English, we change 'I eat' to 'I have eaten', putting in 'have' and changing 'eat' to 'eaten', in Welsh we just put in 'wedi', and leave 'bwyta' or 'darllen' or whatever alone. So now – big exercise! – I want you to have a go at translating the following ten sentences, using first 'yn' and then 'wedi'. Any words you don't know, look them up in the dictionary, or else ask me. Or, of course, ask each other, because I expect you to have picked up some words along the way. And some you've had before, of course.

	yn/'n	wedi
I am eating.		
I am working.		
I'm writing.		
I'm learning Welsh.		
He's going to Cardiff.		
She is sleeping.		
Are you doing the housework?		
I'm thinking about the book.		
Gwilym is drinking coffee.		

Howard: Iawn – dw i wedi ysgrifennu'r geiriau newydd ar y bwrdd.
Mike: You've written what?
Anka: Think it out for yourself, Mike. What is written on the board?
Mike: The new words.
Howard: Mm-hmm.
Mike: Oh. Right. Sorry. Thanks. Oh, er, diolch.
Howard: Océ. Iawn – rŵan ta, ffeindiwch bartner a chymharu'r atebion.
Sally to Rob: *[whispering]* Did he say find a partner and compare the answers?
Rob: I think so! I hope so, cos that's what we're going to do!
Sally: He's started using a lot more Welsh. I feel quite worried. What if we don't understand when he says something important?
Rob: I think he's worked out that we're intelligent enough to either suss it out for ourselves, or check it out with him. You're doing fine. Now, what about these answers?

Coffee time

Howard: How are you all feeling, then?

Anka: I'm enjoying myself.

Howard: Yes, it must help to be used to learning languages. You know you will succeed in the end, even if it's traumatic from time to time! What about you others?

Sally: I feel a bit overwhelmed, to tell the truth.

Howard: When you start learning Welsh, you might sometimes feel a bit overwhelmed – you will be practising the little you know on other people and they will fire a lot back at you – much of which you might not understand. Don't let this get to you! The other person has had a lot more practice than you have! Half the secret of learning a language is persevering. As time goes on, you will understand more and more. And I'm going to be using more and more Cymraeg with you, so you'll hear more here.

Dafydd: Howard, apart from going to classes, and talking to Welsh-speakers, is there any way I can speed up my learning? I don't like to use Welsh-speakers as my guinea-pigs all the time.

Howard: Listen to the language as much as you can – not just actively with tapes and CDs but also passively with the radio. You need to get used to what I call the 'sound system' of the language – the set of Welsh sounds, which will include sounds that don't exist in English, typically the ll and the ch.

Anka: Yes, I've found this with learning any language. Particularly the passive stuff – somehow the language goes into your brain even though you think you're not listening to it!

Howard: In fact, like Anka said earlier, you are dealing with a lot of things – sounds, words, word order in sentences, how to answer questions – both in listen/speak mode and in read/write mode. I think listening as much as possible is very important. There is one school of thought which says that you need to listen quite a lot before even starting to speak. When you think about it, that's how you learned your own mother-tongue – children first hear a lot of language, and only speak when they are ready. I've been building this approach into my teaching more and more over the last few years.

Mike: I like to see the language I'm learning written down, though. Not sure listening to things you don't understand is worthwhile. Sounds daft to me.

Howard: There is no 'perfect' way of learning a language (or anything else, for that matter) – we all learn in different ways – some people are stronger on the visual side, some people need to do things, and others are better learners by just listening. It's important to find out which way suits you best.

Hedd Wyn

This is the statue in Trawsfynydd of the poet Ellis Evans, who used the bardic name 'Hedd Wyn'. He won the bardic chair in the National Eisteddfod in 1917 for his awdl (a long poem in strict metre) that he'd written on the First World War battlefields. News of his win came soon after news of his death reached his family, and at the National Eisteddfod his Chair was draped with black silk, in mourning.

Learner of the Month: Andrew Green

Andrew is the Librarian – THE Librarian, e.g. the boss – at the National Library of Wales – Llyfrgell Genedlaethol Cymru – in Aberystwyth.

'I was born in Lincolnshire and brought up near Sheffield. My mother is a Scot. I've lived in Wales almost continuously since 1973, and my sympathies in priority order are: Wales, Scotland, England.

'I first became aware of Welsh as a living language in the early 1960s. I saw some Welsh TV programmes which were broadcast on weekday afternoons in England, and I remember feeling amazed that people living in the UK, but who had not come from abroad, spoke a first language other than English! After I came to Wales I learnt a smattering of Welsh, but it wasn't until our daughter Catrin was born that I decided I should learn properly. My wife comes from Carmarthen and speaks Welsh, although as a second language, and we both wanted Catrin to grow up Welsh-speaking.

'I also believed that anyone living in Wales should make an attempt to get to grips with the language, in order to have a fuller understanding of the country, and to participate more fully in Welsh life.

'I enrolled on an Wlpan course in Cardiff – a mixed bunch of people, a good tutor, and we met for an hour and a half each day. I worked on after that course ended, and took my GCSE for adult learners in 1989. I got a job in the University in Swansea, where I used my Welsh every day in my job and socially. I applied for my current job in Spring 1998 – the specification said that the post-holder must be highly proficient in both written and oral Welsh. The working language of the Library is Welsh, as you will discover when you visit.

'The language has given me a window into Welsh-language culture of all kinds. I'm convinced that the future of Welsh as a flourishing language depends crucially on its condition as a social, community language, outside and beyond the classroom. It would be pleasant to think that I am living proof that it is possible for non-Welsh-speaking adults to master the language, and, in a small way, contribute to its use on a daily basis.'

Glossary

tatws	potatoes	**Cei**	Quay
pobl	people	**bwrdd**	table/board
y	the	**unrhywun**	anyone
cwm	valley	**arall**	other/else
S4C	Sianel Pedwar Cymru	**gair/geiriau**	word/words
gwleidyddiaeth	politics	**ateb/atebion**	answer (response)/ answers
Yr Alban	Scotland	**cymharu**	to compare
pysgota	fishing	**ysgrifennu**	to write
papur	paper	**plannu**	to plant
newydd/ newyddion	new/news	**astudio**	to study
papur newydd	newspaper	**mwynhau**	to enjoy

Marian wants to know how to say "I love you" in Welsh: "Dw i'n dy garu di."

October/Hydref

The next day of term, I turned up for Year 2 of Wlpan – from Unit 30 – as Val had recommended! Although she had said I 'knew a lot', I felt quite nervous about going into this group, who had been learning for much longer than me.

There was a very different atmosphere in the room – still relaxed, but rather more serious. When people get to the Wlpan Course Year 2, they have already covered the present, past and future tenses, negatives and questions, and what they used to do; they can discuss who owns what, who's who in the family, their health, and tell the time; how to complain about things and illnesses, that sort of thing. All the basics. So starting Year 2 isn't as daunting as starting Year 1, and it's usually the people who are more serious about learning Welsh to a slightly higher standard who have survived and have returned to the fray. I sat down with them – having missed a lot of Year 1 work – and hoped that what I'd learned at the Nant would come back to me – fast!

It was hard starting on Unit 30, without having done Year 1's Units 1 to 29! I'd missed out on a lot of essentials, and although I'd covered some of them at the Nant, there were lots of things I was (and still am!) unsure of. I tried to make time outside classes to go over the units I'd missed, but somehow it never seemed to work. I felt as though I was trying to build a house on foundations of jelly.

I would like to pay tribute to Val. I am sure a lot of my progress was down to her patience and quiet encouragement. We did a lot of laughing. Val is a good tutor in that she doesn't ask too much of people, she is transparent and warm and shares herself with her class, and she praises her learners appropriately.

So much of learning depends on a tutor – but, in the end, it is the learners (particularly adults) who have to take responsibility for their own progress. If we leave it all to the tutor, we are putting all the responsibility into a two-hour lesson once a week, rather than taking the responsibility into our own hands and carrying it with us out of the class and into the street. What we do outside the classroom, I am convinced, makes the difference between moving forward at our own pace, or plodding slowly along at the pace decided by the people who wrote the Wlpan course!

It was a difficult time for me. I was going through a bit of a personal crisis, and I missed a couple of classes. I felt generally despondent, but particularly because I thought I'd never catch up. One day I met Margaret, a classmate from the Wlpan classes in a shop in Aberystwyth, and she asked me if I was all right, because I hadn't been at the class. I told her I thought I'd got too far behind. 'Oh, no, don't feel that! We all feel we're struggling, and we miss you. Do come next time!'

It was so good to hear, and it made all the difference. If it wasn't for Margaret, I might have given up going to Wlpan.

It was crazy. I was struggling with the classes, struggling with the correspondence course, and yet when people sent me e-mails in Welsh, I could read them! More and more, I could read them without the dictionary, or just using it for one or two words. How could this be, if I was such a dunce in other ways?

Then I realised that learning Welsh is not a linear thing when you live in Wales. It isn't just classes. There is such a lot of Welsh around that we're learning all the time. The other people in the class were better than me at mutations, prepositions, possessives, rules – but they didn't get emails in Welsh. So, eventually, we were all going to arrive at the same standard – their accurate Welsh was going to catch up with my 'working Welsh', and vice versa.

So, for the same reasons, it didn't matter if I missed a class, it didn't mean I wasn't going to learn Welsh. It simply meant I'd missed two hours in a classroom!

By the end of October, the personal stuff that had clouded things for me was beginning to get resolved, and Margaret and Val's encouragement had taken some of the stress out of the classes. I decided to plough on – towards the Challenger's deadline …

• Tip of the month

If you are tired, anxious, or unwell, you are likely to feel you are failing – and not just in learning Welsh! Persist! Keep going to the classes! Things are going into your brain – even if you don't think they are, and you can't find them when you want them! You will find them, they are there. Don't give up.

Challenge of the month

Try to find someone to send Welsh e-mails or notes to. Don't worry too much about getting it perfect! Ask for something, and if you get it, you have achieved communication – the aim of language, after all!

 ## Website of the month
http://www.menai.ac.uk/clicclic/

You'll need sound for this! It's a website Howard created, and is very helpful in the early stages of learning.

Wlpan

Wlpan was first devised as a method for teaching Hebrew, when many Jews were leaving other parts of the world and going to live in the young Israel. They needed to learn Hebrew very, very quickly. The government gave them six months of paid leave to learn Hebrew, and the Ulpan courses ran for six hours a day, six days a week. There had to be a structure, and when the Ulpan system came to Wales to teach Welsh (and was called Wlpan), it was modified, but still highly pressurised. Nowadays it is less so, and some tutors are more relaxed than others about the way they run things. For example, some tutors, in the manner of early Ulpan, still don't allow dictionaries in classrooms; many do. Some still do the rapid-fire drilling of the early days; others 'drill' in different, more relaxed, more enjoyable ways, with games and quizzes. Opinions are divided. I much prefer the relaxed, fun ways of learning, and I firmly believe people who are laughing are able to learn better than people who are 'trying hard'.

 ## Book of the month

Kate Roberts – often known as Dr Kate – was one of the most influential literary characters of Wales in the twentieth century. And when I say 'characters', I mean it! She became Wales' foremost short story writer (the first Welsh-language novel didn't appear until the late nineteenth century). They are mostly based in the area where she grew up, around Rhosgadfan near Caernarfon.

There are a number of English-language translations of her books, such as *Feet in Chains* (trans. John Idris Jones, published by John Jones Publishing Ltd). I read these before I could read Welsh, and it's helpful to have the translations available. Kate Roberts' books describe a Cymru (Wales) that is changing, around the beginning of the twentieth century, and they are a record of a way of life that has now largely disappeared. (I have to say, however, that Kate Roberts' Welsh is wonderful, so do plan to graduate to the original versions as soon as you can, even if you don't understand every word.)

You can also find books about Kate Roberts and her great friend Saunders Lewis, and others, in English, which are helpful for understanding the Welsh literary scene of the twentieth century – a time of important developments.

Learning tip – and a 'point to ponder'

Research shows that the best learners of a language are those who are interested in the people who speak that language – their history, their literature, their thinking, and their culture. It is sterile to learn just the language, and far less enjoyable!

Many people believe that the Welsh language is not in danger, because so many adults are learning it, and it's taught in all schools. But this is a dangerous belief, because although the language itself might not be 'in danger', the culture attached to the language is, because so many Welsh-language communities are being diluted, by lack of jobs and housing for young local people. Welsh-speaking people have to leave the area, and incomers move in, taking advantage of cheaper housing. And even if all incomers learned Welsh – and only 60% of incomers have any interest at all in the language! – this still means that the local dialects, songs, stories, relationships etc have fizzled out.

Unfortunately for all of us, learning Welsh is not enough …

But, by learning, we can get involved in Welsh culture, and also support campaigns to strengthen the Welsh language and culture in the Fro Cymraeg – the predominantly Welsh-speaking areas that are fighting for their lives at the moment. Our help is desperately needed!

Welsh Workshop

Marian:	Hi, you-all. Hey, it's getting really good, I can order the dog around in Welsh now!
Sally:	Well done, Marian! Can you order Geraint around in Welsh yet?
Rob:	Don't answer that! Hello, Mike! Has Howard arrived yet?
Howard:	Dw i yma! Bore da! Sut dych chi heddiw?
Marian:	Heddiw? Hang on, dictionary … oh, yes, today. Da iawn, diolch, Howard.
Howard:	Gwych! A chi? Sally, sut dych chi?
Sally:	Da iawn, Howard, diolch. Dw i … er … wedi … oh 'eck … slept well.
Howard:	Iawn – rydych chi wedi cysgu'n dda. Dw i'n falch iawn o glywed hynny. Rob – chi hefyd?
Rob:	Dw i wedi cysgu'n dda … too. Oh, is that 'hefyd'?
Howard:	Dw i'n falch iawn o glywed bod chi wedi cysgu'n dda hefyd. Beth amdanoch chi, Marian?
Marian:	Oh, dw i'n ol reit.
Mike:	Is it all right to say 'ol reit'? It's not really Welsh, is it?
Howard:	Well, you could say, 'Dw i'n iawn'.
Dafydd:	Dw i'n iawn, but I had a bit of a run-in with someone in a shop in town yesterday, because I wanted to speak Welsh with her and she was rude to

Howard: me. I don't think I pronounced something right and she was offended. Well, we'll have to teach you how to say you're sorry, then! Perhaps we'll spend this session looking at some greetings and things you'll need socially. So, let's start with 'I'm sorry'. There are several ways of saying it.

Mae'n ddrwg gynna i.	Mainly in northern areas.
Mae'n ddrwg gen i.	Mainly in the north.
Mae'n flin 'da fi.	Mainly in the south.
Mae'n ddrwg 'da fi.	A mixture of north and south.

Sally: We live near Machynlleth – is that north or south?

Howard: Ah, well, good question! A lot depends on which words you are thinking about, and I find this difficult to answer. Some people say the line runs through Talybont, just north of Aberystwyth. But don't worry too much about the north-south divide – yes, some words happen in the north and not the south, and vice versa, but if you ask for 'llefrith' in the south rather than 'llaeth', if you want milk, you'll get your milk! Now, I've written the apologies on the board. Each of you say them for me. ... Yes, Marian, great. I can tell you live with a Welsh-speaker – you've heard them a lot!

Marian: [laughs] Not from my husband, I can assure you!

Sally: Well, I'm going to make sure Rob learns them!

Rob: I've heard the kids say 'Mae'n drwg gen i' to each other sometimes. Have I said it right?

Howard: Yes, except for the mutated 'd' which is 'dd' – 'mae'n ddrwg', which is the same sound as the 'th' on the front of 'that'. And the 'w' is longer than you've said it. More like the 'ŵ' in dŵr (water) which has a little accent on top. Anyone know what that little accent is called?

Mike: A circumflex?

Howard: That's the technical name, but in Welsh it's called a 'to bach', a little roof! Not to be confused with a 'tŷ bach' – toilet.

Dafydd: I think we all know what one of those is. And while we're on the subject, when is it break time, please?

Howard: Not quite yet! And let's do 'please' while we're at it. Anyone know?

Marian:	Plîs?
Howard:	Er, yes, very commonly used. And since the Welsh 'please' is so long, it's not surprising! 'Os gwelwch yn dda' – 'if you would be so good' is a reasonable English approximation.. And I'll do the 'ti' version too: Os gweli di'n dda'.
Rob:	This 'ti' and 'chi' thing is very confusing.
Anka:	We have it in Slovene. And every other language I've learned, except English.
Howard:	A great many people who learn Welsh as adults are from England, so it's confusing for them. It looks as if most languages have it – but remember that it's not just part of a language, it's part of the culture. When you learn a language, you learn more than just words!
Marian:	You said, greetings. It's Geraint's birthday soon, and I'd love to wish him 'happy birthday' in his own language.
Sally:	Pen … something … hapus, isn't it? I was at a friend's birthday party and they sang it.
Howard:	Pen blwydd hapus. 'Pen' meaning top of, 'blwydd' meaning something to do with a year, and hapus meaning happy! I suppose it's a bit like the Irish saying 'top of the morning'! 'Pen blwydd' is also used in the phrase 'pen blwydd priodas'.
Dafydd:	So what about happy Christmas, then?
Marian:	Nadolig llawen. It's more 'merry' than happy, isn't it. And then there's 'Blwyddyn newydd dda!' for 'happy new year'.
Mike:	What do we say when we meet someone for the first time?
Howard:	Well, you could say, 'Bore da! Braf cwrdd â chi.' Which means, 'I am pleased to meet you.' Or, less formal, 'Neis cwrdd â chi'.
Mike:	And when we want to say 'well done' to someone?
Anka:	Oh, nice long word: 'Llongyfarchiadau!'
Rob:	WHAT?
Anka:	Llongyfarchiadau!
Howard:	It's really 'congratulations', and it's easy enough to say: Llon-gy-farchi-ad-au! And don't forget to stress the penultimate syllable. But you can also just say 'Da iawn!' That's got us nicely off the subject. Let's get back to possession. Let's look at these 'I've got' sentences:

I've got a car.	**Mae gynna i gar.** **Mae car 'da fi.**	North South
I have a brother.	**Mae gynna i frawd.** **Mae brawd 'da fi.**	North South
You've got a problem.	**Mae gynnoch chi broblem.** **Mae problem 'da chi.**	North South

To ask a question, change 'mae' to 'oes': 'Oes gynnoch chi broblem?'
which usually comes out like 'Sgynnoch chi broblem?' Or, more usually in
the south, 'Oes problem 'da chi?'

Mike: Makes life difficult, doesn't it, all these differences between north and
south, and all the differences in word order between Welsh and English.

Anka: Mike, you're always moaning. All languages have different constructions.

Mike: Yes, but English has served me well over the years. Why should I do all
this hard work to speak another language?

Anka: I'll explain it to you later.

Mike: I look forward to that!

Rob: Later?

Anka: Shut up, Rob.

Howard: Interesting! Coffee time now!

Coffee time

Sally: Howard, thanks so much for spending time on pronunciation. I really
don't want to sound English when I'm speaking Welsh.

Howard: Well, Sally, I think that it is important to work on pronunciation for
two reasons: it will be easier for people to understand what you are
saying if you pronouce Welsh well; and it will lower the chances of a
Welsh-speaker switching to English! It's very disheartening to learners
when people switch to English when they realise that the person is a
learner. I guess most of them are trying to be kind (misguidedly); a very

mis 4

few understandably dislike their language being murdered! So good pronunciation will help them, as well as you.

Marian: What should we do? Turn to English too?

Howard: You keep on speaking Welsh. It's you that needs the practice! I remember that when I was little (and not able to speak Welsh), I visited my Welsh-speaking aunt and uncle on the Llŷn Peninsula. One day some friends from a remote farm visited us, and I was surprised that they didn't have a lot of English. If only I could have lived with them for six months! I would have become fluent in Welsh at an early age.

Rob: Our kids have schoolfriends who can't speak any English. That really brought home to me that Welsh is a living language. It's helped our children learn Welsh really fast. And it seems to me that it's a pity they have to learn English. Why not live through Welsh?

Howard: Unfortunately, there are only a few places in Wales now where people can really do that. But learners can help, by encouraging Welsh-speakers to speak Welsh rather than English. And to reduce the chances of people turning to English, one of the things you can do is to work on your pronunciation and accent.

Mike: Anything in particular we should work on?

Howard: Well, particularly, master the ll and ch and also the vowel sounds. For example, the word 'lle' (which can mean either 'where' or 'place', depending on context), can often come out wrongly as 'llay'. And the letter 'o' in Welsh is not pronounced 'oh'! Welsh-speakers say that's a dead give-away, no matter how good someone's Welsh is grammatically. In Welsh words, the stress is usually on the penultimate syllable, although there are exceptions.

Sally: Hmmm. I can see I've been going about this in quite the wrong manner!

Howard: It will come, but be aware of it. As I said, listen to as much Welsh as you can – even if you don't understand it. Also, listen to the way Welsh speakers speak English – the Welsh vowel sounds come out in the English. For example, 'game' is often pronounced as gêm, even in English, particularly in the South Wales valleys.

Learner of the Month: Linda Mary Edwards

Linda Mary is Howard's wife! She is Priest in Charge, looking after the beautiful little church in the tiny village of Pennant Melangell, where St Melangell (Patron Saint of hares) is buried. Also buried there is one of the most famous harpists of the twentieth century, Nansi Richards, also known as 'Telynores Maldwyn'*.

'I was born in Neath, in Glamorgan, with an English mother and a Welsh father. I learned a little Welsh at school, but then started learning properly from the age of 27. I had felt cut off from my roots, because Welsh had been the language of my paternal forefathers and mothers. I wanted to be able to read Welsh literature, and speak to people in Welsh.

'I suppose it took me about three years before I felt reasonably proficient in Welsh. I found mutations difficult, and also knowing which words are male and which are female. There are many different verb forms too. But I tried out my Welsh in Church, in conversations with Welsh colleagues and friends – wherever the opportunity arose. If I'd had someone to speak with daily in Welsh it would have helped, and we didn't have S4C in those days either!

'Now, I love being able to chat to neighbours in Welsh, and to be able to understand better the words of hymns I sang as a child without understanding. I feel I belong.'

* Traditionally, the eminent harpists of Cymru have been named after their counties or areas. A 'telynores' is a female harpist. Nansi Richards, from Sir Faldwyn – Montgomeryshire, in English – was perhaps the most innovative harpist of the twentieth century. She played well into her 80s, and features on several CDs of Welsh folk music.

Glossary

llaeth/llefrith	milk	lle (g), ble (d)	where
dŵr	water	gogledd	north
to bach	little roof = circumflex accent	de	south
os gweli di'n dda	please (familiar)	blwyddyn	year
pen blwydd	birthday	priodas	marriage
hapus	happy	neis	nice
Nadolig	Christmas	llongyfarchiadau	congratulations
llawen	merry	brawd	brother
da iawn	very good	cwrdd	to meet

Llywelyn Ein Llyw Olaf *(see page 88)*

Prince Llywelyn Ein Llyw Olaf (*our last leader*) – in many people's view the last true Prince of Wales – was killed by an English lancer in 1282 and his head paraded round London on a pole. This stone, in Cilmeri, near Builth Wells, commemorates where he was captured.

November / *Tachwedd*

November was a long month of ups and downs. I still felt as if I was running up a down escalator. My brain felt clogged. But I was determined to keep going, with Wlpan two mornings a week, and the correspondence course, and everything else ... it was just that I wasn't sure where I was going!

One big mistake I made was to begin to ignore the mutations in Welsh. It was partly due to missing Wlpan Units 1-29, partly due to my own laziness, and partly because Welsh-speakers said, 'Don't worry about mutations, they're not really important.'

That was reassuring, then – one pressure I could remove from my brain – except that it was partly wrong.

I think it's all right to say, 'Don't worry about the mutations' as in, don't lie awake in the middle of the night feeling useless, unable to get the hang of them. Don't be 'disabled' by them, and most of all, DON'T let mutations stop you learning Welsh. Many people do give up because of mutations. They can make you feel so stupid! There are many rules for when to use them and when not to; some words can begin with any one of three different letters, depending on the situations; and when it comes to looking things up in a dictionary – well, that's possibly the most frustrating of all. But it's sad that such a small thing as this can deprive so many people of going on to proficiency in Welsh.

Mutations are to do with the way a language is spoken. Mutations smooth off the rough edges of a language. We need them for the flow of this wonderful language. Welsh without the mutations has been described as 'like a machine gun' by a Welsh-speaker friend of mine. You CAN communicate without them, but if you want to speak good Welsh, and have your Welsh enjoyed by the Cymry Cymraeg, then it's worth working a bit harder.

Trouble is, Welsh mutations, while being to do with the spoken language, are also part of written Welsh! And that is to do with Welsh being a phonetic language – WYSIWYG – what you see is what you get. And what you hear is also what you get, written down.

So, we're lumbered with 'em.

If, unlike me, you learn the rules early on, you'll get mutations right much earlier. I'm still trying! I still don't know all the rules. I wish I did. I'm trying to apply myself, but if only I hadn't so gladly side-stepped them!

• Language tip of the month

If 'don't worry about the mutations' means 'don't upset yourself about them', then fine.

But if 'don't worry' becomes 'don't bother', then that's laziness (like mine), and I can't recommend it!

Television programme of the month

The Sunday night hymn singing programme – *Dechrau Canu, Dechrau Canmol* ('Start to Sing, Start to Praise') – is very useful for beginners. You get the Welsh words on screen, and if you try to sing them, and listen at the same time, you find out a lot about pronunciation of Welsh. Don't put the English subtitles on at the same time! At this stage don't worry too much about what you're singing about. As you go further with your learning you will learn to appreciate the beauty of the hymns, particularly some of the older ones.

Website of the month

www.gwybodiadur.co.uk

This website is a tremendous resource for anyone learning the language, or thinking about doing so. But it is possible (as with any website) that some of the information might be out of date. Still worth a trawl round, though!

Book of the month

Real Wales Heini Gruffudd (Y Lolfa £4.95)

A gem of a book. A tiny potted Cymru! Whether you are thinking of moving here, or have done, but don't know much about us, you'll find something here. It's written in a lively way, and it contains – well – loads! Welsh-language rock music sits side by side with pre-Celtic burial chambers; there are myths, controversies, and politics. And all this for £4.95! (Published by Y Lolfa.)

 # Welsh Workshop

Mike: Hello, Dafydd! I thought I'd be late this morning because of the fog, but it was only patchy. What's 'patchy' in Welsh, I wonder?

Anka: Here's a dictionary. You could look it up. If that's not too much bother.

Mike: Ooh, sarcasm! What's that in Welsh? Oops – here's Howard. Bore da, Howard.

Howard: Bore da! Ydych chi wedi cael brecwast y bore 'ma? Sut oedd e?

Anka: Dim yn ddrwg, diolch.

Dafydd: Eh? Oh, gwych, I reckon.

Anka: Dw i'n colli bwyd Slofenaidd.

Rob: I'm lost. Colli?

Anka: To lose. Or in my case, to miss.

Dafydd: Oh! I see now! My Nan in Ponty used to say she'd lost the bus instead of she'd missed it!

Howard: Yes, there are a lot of constructions like that in English down south. Now you know where they're from!

Sally: But Howard, you said something about brecwast that I didn't understand. Sut something.

Howard: Sut oedd brecwast. Yes, oedd. It's part of what's called the imperfect tense – a term I don't like, so I prefer to call it the 'was/were' tense. We've done the present tense, and the 'wedi' tense. So now let's look at 'was/were'! I've written this on the board for you.

Dw i'n darllen llyfr. I am reading a book.	**Rôn i'n darllen llyfr.** I was reading a book.
Wyt ti'n gyrru car. You are driving a car	**Rôt ti'n gyrru car.** You were driving a car.
Mae Glenys yn neidio. Glenys is jumping.	**Roedd Glenys yn neidio.** Glenys was jumping.
Dyn ni'n gweithio. We are working.	**Roedden ni'n gweithio.** We were working.
Dych chi'n canu. We are singing.	**Roedden ni'n canu.** We were singing.
Maen nhw'n cusanu. They are kissing.	**Roedden nhw'n cusanu.** They were kissing.

Mike:	Cusanu. Must remember that for future reference! Might come in very handy!
Howard:	Eh? … Erm … moving on … can you see clearly the differences between the two tenses?
Rob:	Yes, thanks, it's very clear. But I can also see that there's something wrong with Anka. Are you all right? You're very red. Are you too hot?
Sally:	Shut UP, Rob.
Mike:	She's fine, Rob.
Rob:	Well, I'm only concerned …
Sally:	SHUT UP!
Anka:	[giggles] I'm fine, thank you, Rob.
Howard:	Glad to hear it. Hmm. So – now, negative statements. Anyone know how we make 'Rw i'n darllen llyfr' into a negative?
Marian:	I'm sure 'dim' comes into it somewhere.
Howard:	Yes, but where?
Marian:	Dw i'n dim darllen llyfr?
Howard:	Close, but remember that 'yn' relates to 'darllen'.

Marian:	Oh – Dw i dim yn darllen llyfr.
Howard:	Da iawn! Just one small tweak: it's 'Dw i ddim'.
Mike:	So 'Dw i' is positive and 'Dw i ddim' is negative.
Rob:	Ah, then it's 'Dw i ddim yn darllen llyfr' – is that right?
Howard:	Da iawn. Gwych. Rŵan 'ta, go with the sentences on the board, and let's see how you get on. Who's going to start? Anka?
Anka:	Dwyt ti ddim yn gyrru car – ?
Howard:	Iawn – nesa?
Sally:	Oh …
Howard:	Here, 'mae' changes to 'dydy' with 'ddim'.
Sally:	… right. Dydy Glenys ddim yn neidio.
Rob:	Dyn ni ddim yn gweithio.
Mike:	Dych chi ddim yn canu.
Marian:	Dydyn nhw ddim yn cusanu.
Mike:	What's 'later' yn y Gymraeg?
Howard:	Eh? Oh, 'yn hwyrach'.
Rob:	Why do you ask?
Sally:	Rob, shut up and stop being so blasted tactless!
Rob:	Eh?
Howard:	Don't worry, Rob, I'm lost too. Now, I want you to make a similar table, using different verbs. Try hard not to refer to this stuff on the board at all while you're doing it – try to work it out for yourselves. And then, get together with the others and see how you've done.

Your turn!

Positive statement	'was/were' tense statement	Negative statement
Dw i'n canu cân. I am singing a song.	**Rôn i'n canu cân.** I was singing a song.	**Dw i ddim yn canu cân.** I am not singing a song.

Rwyt ti'n hapus. You are happy.		
Mae Idris yn gweithio. Idris is working.		
Mae Siân yn darllen. Sian is reading.		
Mae hi'n cysgu. She is sleeping.		
Dyn ni'n bwyta. We are eating.		
Dych chi'n lwcus. You are lucky.		
Maen nhw'n ymlacio. They are relaxing.		

Coffee time

Rob: Howard, how many sounds are there in Welsh that don't occur in English?

Howard: Quite a few. And there are some Welsh sounds that do not occur in standard English, but might occur in dialect English. Many Welsh vowel sounds are 'straight'. In standard English, the 'a' in 'same' starts with a sound similar to the 'e' in 'egg' and ends like the first 'e' in 'theme'. It 'glides' from one to the other. In Yorkshire, it doesn't glide like this. It is a 'straight' sound. This is how 'ê' is pronounced in Welsh. In written Welsh, we use 'accents' like the circumflex – or 'to bach' – to show that the vowel sound is lengthened. The borrowed word 'game' is an example. In Welsh it is pronounced as 'gêm' – similar to the Geordie way of pronouncing it. The 'to bach' elongates the vowel sound. It can make a big difference to the meaning of words like these:

gêm = game   **gem** = jewel   (the g is not pronounced like the j)
ffôn = telephone   **ffon** = stick
glân = clean   **glan** = bank (as in river bank – not the financial kind!)

However, some words with a longish vowel don't have a 'to bach'. The one Welsh sound that never occurs in English is the double-l – 'll' as in 'llan'. Mind you, the 'ch', which sounds similar to the 'ch' in Scottish 'loch', turns up in Liverpudlian English!

Mike: Is Welsh the only language with the 'll' sound?

Howard: No, certainly some African languages have it. In the Welsh alphabet, the 'll' is classified in its own right.

Mike: I don't think I'm doing 'll' right. How do I say it?

Howard: Put your tongue behind your upper front teeth, keep it there, and blow out past one side of your tongue ... That's it! Perffaith!

Mike: Is that really all there is to it? Everyone thinks it's difficult.

Howard: Nope, not difficult at all. Many languages also have a 'ch' sound. You need to make it in the back of your mouth. Rob and Sally, you have the perfect example in 'Machynlleth'.

Sally: Oh! I've always pronounced it like 'Muh-hynlleth'! I need to gargle more!

Howard: Well done! You can practise a lot on place names.

Rob: Yes, some of them look really odd at first, but now I know a bit about how to pronounce them, they're fine! I'm looking forward to being able to say that long Welsh place name on Ynys Môn! Someone told me it isn't really Welsh, though.

Howard: It is Welsh, but a concocted name, but that's another story! Going back to gliding vowel sounds, Welsh has them, but they are represented by double vowels on paper.

Rob: Right – like Geraint ... and Heini, which I see means 'fit', but it's also the name of the bloke that wrote this Learners' Dictionary! Odd name, 'Fit Gruffudd'.

Howard: 'Tis, isn't it. I've often wondered about that.

Learner of the month: Rhian Roberts

Rhian lives near Caernarfon in Gwynedd.

'I was born and brought up in South Wales. My father spoke Welsh, though he never did so with the family. My mother was born in England. She never tried to learn Welsh. At school 'Welsh' was a subject, alongside other subjects. I did Welsh as a second language at A-Level, but the emphasis was on writing and reading Welsh rather than speaking.

'In my gap year, I worked as a Mother's Help with a Welsh-speaking family, and that was my first experience of people with Welsh as a 'first language'. I could soon say simple, everyday things in Welsh, but my range was limited.

'I went to University in England, but even then Welsh was important to me. I went to Nant Gwrtheyrn several times prior to moving back in 2002 (after 25 years). I did some one-to-one sessions with a native Welsh-speaker, which helped a lot. When I came to live here, I made a point of using my Welsh whenever it was possible – you have to be willing to give it a go even when it feels difficult or embarrassing.

I also chose jobs where I knew Welsh would be used on a daily basis. I carried on with Welsh classes.

'Even after nearly 40 years, there are still occasions where I feel that I can say anything I want to in Welsh, but other times when I realise that I don't know exactly how to say something. One thing that makes Welsh difficult to learn is that because English is so prevalent and because everyone can speak English, it is difficult to be 'immersed' in Welsh, as one can be immersed in French in France, or in Spanish in Spain. It helps if you can get people to speak Welsh in your presence, and explain things in Welsh, rather than turning to English.

'The more I speak Welsh the more I enjoy it, and the more I appreciate it as an extremely beautiful language. I have come to respect those for whom Welsh is truly a 'mother-tongue', and to realise how important it is to safeguard and develop the language. The whole world of Welsh literature, poetry and culture becomes increasingly available. Most importantly, of course, non-Welsh speakers moving into predominantly Welsh-speaking areas need to be aware of how damaging their refusal to learn Welsh and their use of English is, especially in communities where Welsh has always been the first language of the indigenous population.'

Glossary

ffon	stick	**brecwast**	breakfast
bwyd	food	**ffôn**	phone
Slofenaidd	Slovenian	**canu**	to sing
sut	how	**canmol**	to praise
llyfr	book	**ymlacio**	to relax
hwyr/yn hwyrach	late/later	**cusanu**	to kiss
lwcus	lucky	**neidio**	to jump
cân	song	**colli**	to miss/to lose
glan	bank of river	**cael**	to have
glân	clean	**dechrau**	to start/the start
gem	gemstone	**lolfa**	living room
gêm	game		

Roedden ni'n gallu ymlacio yn Fenis.

December/*Rhagfyr*

Through November and into December, I carried on with classes. My personal problems diminished and I had more concentration, and an urge to move on fast. I had a week in Venice (our 'summer holiday'), and took the correspondence course with me. I did two units of written work, and prepared the scripts ready to record two tapes when I got home.

Missing two classes was more of a problem. I took the Wlpan book with me, and tried to understand what was going on in my absence. But a good thing with Wlpan is that if you're not in the class, you've got an idea about the content of the class, because you have the book.

When I got back to Ceredigion, I joined classes again – just in time for the end of term! That's a big disadvantage – in Aberystwyth, at least, the courses follow the University terms, so there are huge breaks. People worry that they'll lose their Welsh. CYD, the learners' society, too, with their groups of Welsh-speakers mixing with learners, follow the University terms, which means you don't get much conversation practice over the breaks. Particularly for people in their first years of Welsh, and people with no Welsh-speaking friends or family, there is no practice at all for something like six weeks over Christmas, three over Easter, and about ten over the summer!

It seems like a dead stop.

However, I was, unexpectedly, relieved. The clogging in my brain had intensified. I couldn't speak Welsh. When I tried to, I dried up.

It would have been frightening, had I not known it is part of the process of learning a language. But it's another point at which it is easy to feel totally demoralised and to want to crawl under a stone. And the 'going back to school' feeling at the beginning of a new term, after such a long break, can be enough to make some people not return to classes.

I knew that what I needed was time to myself, when I could sit with the coursework and unravel the mess in my head. But what are we all like before Christmas? Frantic! So it had to wait. And I just had to hope it would work out! Unfortunately I'm a natural pessimist, and so I was completely convinced I'd lost the ability to learn Welsh. I met my Challenger for a meal, but we didn't speak even a word of Welsh all evening! I couldn't speak it, or understand it. Fortunately, he understands the process of learning a language, and he didn't try to make me speak. I kept thinking back to the Nant summer course, and being so confident at the end of the fortnight. In my more positive times I allowed myself to be pleased and buoyed up by that.

In my less positive times, the Nant seemed to be mocking me ...

And to make matters worse, the two correspondence course units I'd done in Venice came back ... oh, woe ... so many errors! In fact, I was so miserable about it that I threw it on a pile and left it for several weeks. When I eventually came to analyse it, there were basically three errors, repeated many times: the incorrect (or no) use of 'yn'; forgetting to use a singular noun immediately after a number (I still forget that!); and MUTATIONS – millions and millions of them.

Don't get me wrong. I didn't for a moment feel annoyed with my tutor, only with myself. I'd been working in a sloppy, slapdash way, in order to move on fast, and it hadn't paid off. It was time to pull myself together. A New Year. A new resolve!

 **Website of the Month**

www.gtj.org.uk

"Gathering the Jewels" is the English name for this site – 20,000 images of photos, books, letters and objects from museums, record offices and libraries throughout Wales.

Learning tip

We're not at school, we're adults – therefore, we need to take responsibility for our own learning. A tutor can do only so much in an hour, two hours, whatever. The rest of the time it's down to us.

 Book of the month

Singing in Chains Mererid Hopwood (Gomer, £8.99)

Mererid made history by being the first woman to win the bardic Chair at the National Eisteddfod, back in 2001. The title is taken from one of Dylan Thomas' finest poems, Fernhill, and shows that even those writing poetry in English can use cynghanedd. But it is primarily a Welsh-language form. The word means 'harmony', and Mererid shows in this readable book how it is used. There is a CD to go with the book. Highly recommended!

11 December: Dydd Llywelyn yr Ail – Llywelyn II's Day

Llywelyn ap Gruffudd (1225-1282) was the last Prince of Wales. His successes against England led Edward I (Longshanks) to build a number of castles in Wales, designed to subdue and disadvantage the Welsh. (By the way, don't think for a moment that castles such as Caerffili, Caernarfon etc are 'Welsh castles'. Far from it! There was a great chain of Edward's castles, and Welshmen and their families were not able to live within the walls. For true Welsh castles, look at Dolwyddelan, Castell y Bere, and others.) Llywelyn fought Edward in two wars of independence, and on 11 December 1282, he was killed at Cilmeri, near Builth Wells. His body was buried in Cwmhir Abbey, and his head was paraded round London. There is a huge memorial stone to him at Cilmeri, and on this day each year, patriots meet there to remember him.

Website of the month 2

www.museumwales.ac.uk

Lots of information about the museums of Wales, and lots of information too about the research that is attached to them. There is a lot more about the history of the National Eisteddfod, for example, than I have put into this book. If you can, go to the Museum of Welsh Life at St Fagan's near Cardiff. It's a lovely day out (especially if the weather is good), and you will learn a lot. The guides in the houses speak Welsh, and are full of enthusiasm for the particular building they are working in. The buildings have been moved from all over Cymru, and are furnished accordingly.

Christmas: go to a Plygain service

If you get a chance, go to a Plygain service. They are held around Christmas, and mainly in mid-Wales, although in a few places they are held on Christmas morning: this is the traditional time for the plygain.

The custom was for the young people either to stay awake the night before Christmas, or to get up early – sometimes as early as 2am! They would party until the plygain, decorating the house with holly or mistletoe, and in some places making toffee – there is a recipe on the Museum of Welsh Life website, www. museumwales.ac.uk/en/277/, together with lots of other information. In some areas they would make special candles, and the churches would blaze with light – symbolic of the coming of the Light of the World.

Although churches are now lit by electricity, there is a feeling of being very much in touch with history in a plygain service. Taking part is interesting. Each 'party' should have at least three carols ready, because the rule is that if someone else sings one that you were going to sing, you can't sing it! After an introduction, everyone sits and waits, and then the first 'party' comes to the front and sings one of the traditional plygain carols, some centuries old. Then they return to their seats and someone else is ready to sing. There is no 'order of singing' – you just choose your moment and go to the front. There are mixed choirs, individuals, and groups of varying sizes. The farmer and his son. A group of young men who look as if they've just come off the rugby pitch. A married couple. An old man. Sometimes a child. No fuss, no drama, just an ancient story being told in song, just as it has been since the sixteenth century, perhaps earlier.

When every 'party' has sung, there is a congregational hymn, and then each 'party' sings their second song, in the same order of singing. There is no written order of 'performance', you need to remember who you sang after the first time round, and follow them in the second half!

At the end of the service, all the men singers go to the front and sing a song exhorting everyone to enjoy the refreshments that have been prepared. Traditionally the men sang all the carols while the women made the refreshments – and although beer used to be drunk instead of tea, and although quite a few of the 'parties' are now mixed, it still appears to be the women who make the cakes and sandwiches! Wonderful spreads, which are all part of the worship.

Try to find a plygain service near you, or travel further afield. It's worth it. Even if you don't understand any of the Welsh (and remember, a lot of it is in dialects, so it's not even easy for first-language Welsh speakers), it is an important part of the culture of the land you live in.

 # Welsh Workshop

Rob:	Phew, I'm exhausted! I had a really bad night.
Sally:	So did I. There was a big party in our village, and someone was playing bongos outside our window until about 3am. Playing loudly.
Howard:	Yn Gymraeg, os gwelwch yn dda!
Sally:	Oh. Er ... Roedd rhywun yn ... er ... playo?
Howard:	Yn chwarae.
Sally:	... yn chwarae bongos tu allan ein ffenest tan tua thri a.m. Beth ydy 'a.m.' yn y Gymraeg?
Howard:	tri y.b. – tri y bore. Iawn! Good try! And 'playing loudly'?
Sally:	Yn chwarae ... no, no idea, sorry.
Howard:	Well, this is good, cos Mike asked me if we can look at adverbs in this session!
Dafydd:	Mike did?

Mike: Yeah, me. Why not?

Anka: Ooh, Mike, I'm impressed!

Howard: Océ. Adverbs. They are quite simple really, but we're going to combine them with some revision of what we've already done, and some other bits and pieces. So. Loud is what, Marian-with-the-dictionary!

Marian: Ah – swnllyd.

Howard: Iawn. So, here it is then: 'Roedd rhywun yn chwarae yn swnllyd'. The 'yn' before the 'swnllyd' is equivalent to the 'ly' in English. Like 'siaradwch yn araf; – speak slowly'. Give me some more adjectives relating to music.

> **quiet**   **fast**   **slow**

Da iawn. Rŵan ta …

Anka: Howard, sorry to interrupt, but why do you say 'rŵan ta' instead of 'nawr te'?

Marian: Because that's correct. Isn't it, Howard?

Howard: Ah, well, if you're from the north it might be! If you're from the south, it is less usual. It's 'one of those'. You can use either, depending who you're talking to. 'Rŵan ta' is dominant in the north, 'nawr te' in the south. There's nothing wrong with a northern person saying 'rŵan ta' in Caerdydd, nothing at all. After all, in England, Geordies aren't going to modify their use of words if they travel south, are they?

Mike: I like a simple life. I'll just use your northern version and ignore the other. What's the point of learning both?

Anka: The point, Mike, is that it's nice to be able to communicate with someone in the language or dialect that they speak. I've learned 'nawr te'. So learn both, and you can communicate with me.

Mike: I haven't noticed a problem so far.

Howard: Er … as I was saying. Let's look at adverbs in Welsh. Like with 'yn swnllyd', you put 'yn' in front. So, back to your list, and I'll write the Welsh versions on the board. And remember that some words mutate after 'yn'.

quiet	quietly	fast	fast/quickly	slow	slowly
distaw	**yn ddistaw**	**cyflym**	**yn gyflym**	**araf**	**yn araf**
tawel	**yn dawel**				

Howard: So there you are. Just remember the 'yn'. What about applying these to the weather? That's a really important thing to learn! It just starts, 'mae hi'n' almost all the time in the present tense. Does anyone know any ways of saying what the weather is doing?

Marian: [laughs] Yes, well, I've heard Geraint saying some things on the farm, but I don't think they're repeatable.

Howard: Right – let's do the repeatable stuff! Give me a brainstorm – what sorts of weather are there? I'll write them on the board. Fine … terrible… cloudy … sunny … pouring with rain … fog … snow … frost … hot … windy … cold. All weather terms. So here they are in a table, with the Welsh present tense sentence:

Your suggestions	Nouns	Adjectives	Sentence – 'It is …'
fine	-	braf	Mae'n braf.
terrible	-	ofnadwy	Mae'n ofnadwy.
cloudy	cwmwl	cymylog	Mae'n gymylog.
sunny	haul	heulog	Mae'n heulog.
rain	glaw	-	Mae'n bwrw glaw.
fog	niwl	niwlog	Mae'n niwlog.
snow	eira	-	Mae'n bwrw eira.
frost	rhew	rhewllyd	Mae'n rhewllyd.
hot	-	poeth	Mae'n boeth.
windy	gwynt	gwyntog	Mae'n wyntog.
cold		oer	Mae'n oer.

	You can see the 'yn' there, in all of them. 'It is [in the state of] braf.
Anka:	And 'bwrw', Howard, what does that mean? 'Mae'n bwrw glaw.'
Howard:	This is one of many Welsh words that has a lot of possibilities! Like Welsh weather!
Marian:	The Geiradur Mawr says, 'to cast, to strike, to rain, to count, to suppose, to spend'!
Howard:	And it can mean 'to throw' too. 'It's throwing rain' is nice!
Marian:	Am I allowed to say that Geraint says, 'Mae'n pisho lawr'?
Howard:	Yeah, why not! Very commonly used, if not conventionally taught in classes!
Mike:	And useful. Specially here. Pisses down a lot here, usually when I'm fishing.
Anka:	Oh, come on, Mike. We have lots of sun. It was lovely last Sunday, wasn't it?
Rob:	Why? What happened last Sunday?
Mike:	How do you say, 'It was sunny', Howard?
Howard:	Roedd hi'n heulog. Hmm… what *did* happen last Sunday?
Anka:	Nothing, Howard… nothing at all!

Mae'n stormus yn
Aberystwyth heddiw!

Coffee time

Mike: You know me by now, Howard – always trying to make learning Welsh easy for myself! How many words are there in Welsh that we know already? I think they're called 'borrowed words'.

Howard: There are quite a lot of Welsh words that are quite similar to English ones. For example, lots of words that end in –et in English become words that end in –ed in Welsh, like pocket – poced, carpet – carped, and rocket – roced.

Sally: I've seen 'miwsig' for 'music' – is that an acceptable ending too?

Howard: Yes, English words ending in –ic can go to –ig or –eg in Welsh: clinic – clinig, garlic – garlleg, tonic – tonig, music – miwsig. Yes, that's fine. And also, words that end in –ing in English can end in –in in Welsh, like landing (top of stairs) – landin, and paving – pafin.

Marian: And pudding becomes pwdin! Like, pwdin Dolig!

Rob: What about putting 'o' on the end of verbs? What do you think of that? Is that OK?

Howard: Well, yes, you can do that. Some verbs like that have become acceptable as Welsh words, but it can get out of hand and become rather irritating to some people. For example, 'cicio' – to kick – is OK; 'cnocio' – to knock – is OK, but 'deseidio' – to decide – ych a fi! And 'endio i fyny' – to end up – ych a fi!

Rob: So how do you say 'to end up' in Welsh, then?

Howard: Be very careful here! Sometimes you can't do a direct translation, and you end up with something that sounds at best very inelegant, and at worst absolutely dreadful!

Anka: To change the subject a bit, what about 'Cymraeg' and 'Cymreig'? I've seen them both around, but what's the difference?

Howard: 'Cymraeg' – pronounced with the 'raeg' like 'raag' or 'raheeg' – is to do with the language – in fact, it is the language – 'yr Iaith Gymraeg' – the

Welsh language. 'Cymreig' is more general, and to do with anything that is Welsh – 'bwyd Cymreig' (Welsh food).

Anka: Oh, thanks, that helps. And thinking about it, it's the same with other nations in Welsh, like 'Ffrangeg' for the French language, but 'Ffrengig' for something French.

Dafydd: What about English and the English?

Howard: The English language is 'Saesneg'. Something English is 'Seisnig'. An Englishman is 'Sais', an Englishwoman is a 'Saesnes', and English people in general are 'Saeson'.

Marian: And Geraint is a 'Cymro', I know that. What are you, Howard?

Howard: Cymro ydw i! And you have 'Cymraes' for a Welshwoman, and the Welsh people in general are the Cymry.

Rob: What about the Germans?

Howard: We haven't got time now – end of coffee time – you can look them up and let us know next time! And all the other nationalities and languages too! That's your homework!

Mmm… dw i'n hoffi 'Dolig!

Learner of the Month: Tim Webb

Tim is a Priest in the Church in Wales

'I got interested in the Welsh and Gaelic languages when camping with my family. Later, in 1975, I came to University in Aberystwyth to do Geography and French, but as I had to take three subjects in the first year, I

signed on to 'Welsh for Beginners'. I was told, 'If you're thinking of learning Welsh, go and live in Neuadd Pantycelyn' – the Hall of Residence for Welsh-speakers!

'I shared a room with a Welsh-speaker. I asked him to speak nothing but Welsh to me, but he wouldn't have spoken English to me anyway! The whole idea of Neuadd Pantycelyn is for students to be able to live as much of their lives as possible through Welsh. I went to the Cŵps [Cooper's Arms in Aberystwyth] and, listening to the folk singing there, I realised there is more to Welsh than just the language. I got more and more hooked on the language and its culture, and joined the male voice choir for the inter-college Eisteddfod.

'This was the time of the roadsigns protests [when people were trying to get roadsigns in both Welsh and English – at the time they were in English only or English first]. At first I criticised the campaign, but I gradually understood that something radical had to be done. At the end of the first year I dropped French and Geography and changed my degree to Celtic Studies. I then joined Cymdeithas yr Iaith Gymraeg [the Welsh Language Society] at the start of Year 2, and got involved in protests and pickets.

'The second year was a difficult and rather lonely time for me, because I had enough Welsh to get by, but not enough to get deep, and I nearly gave up. However, I got a summer job on a farm near Aberystwyth, with a Welsh-speaking family. Everyone, from the grandmother to the children, spoke Welsh to me the whole time – very 'Cardi' Welsh, and it did the trick! The farmer was a JP – I subsequently appeared before him when Cymdeithas ran a campaign to get British Rail to use the Welsh language, and a group of us refused to pay our train fare. (We won the campaign!) By the beginning of my third year at University I had crossed the bridge linguistically, and was gradually getting there culturally and psychologically. I took part in a number of protests and campaigns for Cymdeithas, including breaking into holiday homes and climbing a television mast. I spent a week in Swansea Prison, and received a one-year suspended sentence for another protest.

'I don't regret any of this, but there is still much to be done to secure a future for the Welsh language and culture – if anything (contrary to the official line), the crisis has deepened. However, while I still consider that law-breaking is justified in certain circumstances, I do think that it should be used more carefully and sparingly perhaps than I did in the 1970s and '80s!'

Mae'r tywydd yn dda, ac mae'r artist yn tynnu llun castell.

Glossary

tonic	tonig	**yr ail**	second
plygain	matins	**landin**	landing
ffenest	window	**pafin**	pavement
tan	until	**braf**	fine
y bore	the morning/a.m.	**oer**	cold
yn swnllyd	noisily	**cwmwl/cymylog**	cloud/cloudy
distaw/yn ddistaw	silent/silently	**haul/heulog**	sun/sunny
tawel/yn dawel	quiet/quietly	**glaw**	rain
cyflym/yn gyflym	fast/quickly	**niwl/niwlog**	fog/foggy
araf/yn araf	slow/slowly	**eira**	snow
stormus	stormy	**rhew/rhewllyd**	frost/frosty
poced	pocket	**poeth**	hot
carped	carpet	**gwynt/gwyntog**	wind/windy
roced	rocket	**cnocio**	to knock
clinig	clinic	**malu**	to grind
garlleg	garlic	**cicio**	to kick
ofnadwy	awful		

January/*Ionawr*

After Christmas, I had a few weeks to start going through my notes before classes began again. I still hadn't caught up with Units 1-29! Unit 10 seemed to be particularly important: the Possessives – 'his car' – ei gar e; 'their children' – eu plant nhw, and so on.

There was a guy, Gwyn, in my group who was doing Units 1-29 on Mondays and Wednesdays, and Units 30-62 on Tuesdays and Thursdays – four mornings a week! Gwyn was dead keen. He'd retired from work. After his classes, he'd go home and listen to Radio Cymru and struggle with Welsh novels and the papur bro (see 'Book of the Month'). He has immersed himself in Welsh and is making great headway.

Listening to Welsh radio is great. Even if you don't understand everything, you will find yourself being able to understand the odd word here and there, and then you'll find yourself knowing what the news headlines are about, and then you'll understand one or two of the news items, or something on a phone-in. And one day you'll find yourself laughing at one of the jokes!

We all need indications of progress, and since there are no exams attached to Wlpan, we have to look elsewhere. Papurau bro and radio are two of the best places to look!

After I'd sat with the coursework for a day or so, the fog in my head began to clear. (Fogs do, in time.) One of the greatest regrets now is that I didn't do the Wlpan homework. Every Unit has a sheet of homework. I ignored it. I always intended to do it, but never did. That would have helped me a lot – and perhaps avoided some of the fog.

I then looked, reluctantly, at the next units in the correspondence course, and, still feeling defeated and stupid, put it away again.

Then at the end of January, back to the classes. People struggling to recall their Welsh after several weeks of none, or very little. Others, who had Welsh partners, or who worked in a Welsh-speaking environment were further on than when we'd broken up for Christmas. Again I valued and admired Val as she scraped up this motley crew into some kind of a cohesive class. With an eye still on 1 September, I found I was beginning to concentrate better on my own learning, and to be less distracted by other learners. It was no longer 'my' problem. What was my problem was beating The Challenge. No-one could do it for me. No-one could make it easier. And no-one was going to get in the way of my beating it. So I had to work, and work damn hard. I had 7 months – February to the end of August. Time to go up another gear.

• Tip of the Month

The Cadw Sŵn Welsh Course, by Colin Jones. This is a course you can do at home, in your own time, with characters and stories in Welsh on CDs. The texts are in parallel, Welsh and English. You hear the Welsh while you see the English. The method uses classical music (well played!), and the overall effect is that the words and grammar are absorbed unconsciously. This method really works!
www.cadwswn.com

Book of the month

Papur bro: area paper. Every Welsh-speaking area has one. It's a very local news sheet, compiled by local people, all in Welsh. Some of them carry very local news like Aunty Bron's passed her driving test at last, and Ffred has just come out of

hospital after his piles operation and is feeling much better! Papurau bro are well worth picking up. They are usually monthly. The articles are short, and the Welsh isn't too literary, though sometimes a little formal. Also, it will be the Welsh of the area you are living in. The more you struggle with things like your papur bro, the sooner you will find yourself being able to read it!

 **Website of the month**

cs.cf.ac.uk/fun/welsh

This is a Welsh course for you to do on your own. Though you might be going to classes, it is always good to do more work on your Welsh. Let me know how you get on!

Customs: Yr Hen Galan

In many areas of Wales, groups of children would go from house to house on New Year's Eve collecting Calennig (New Year's gifts). They would sing a song at the door, or say verses, and would carry apples stuck with ears of corn and sprigs of greenery. They would receive small gifts of food or money. Something like 'trick or treating' without the tricks!

Also around New Year, or Christmas, and mostly in the south of the country, there was a tradition of going round houses with the Mari Lwyd – the grey mare. A horse's skull would be decorated with ribbons and put on a stick carried by a man, with a sheet over him. With the Mari Lwyd too, songs were sung outside the door, and those inside would need to reply in another verse of the song – often made up – to keep the Mari Lwyd out. (Singing competitions of various types were – and still are – a big part of the musical culture of Cymru.) When eventually admitted to a house, the mare would rush round snapping its teeth at the girls in the house!

Sometimes this would all happen on the Old New Year's Day – Dydd Hen Galan. In 1753, the calendar was changed, but in some areas people kept Dydd Hen Galan, in the middle of January. Some places still have parties on Dydd Calan Go Iawn – the real New Year's Day – and sometimes go from house to house as before.

25 January: Dydd Santes Dwynwen – St Dwynwen's Day

More and more of us in Wales are commemorating Dydd Santes Dwynwen, rather than St Valentine's Day. Dwynwen was said to be one of 24 daughters of Brychan Brycheiniog, Brychan of Brecon. She was both religious and beautiful. Maelon Gwynedd fell in love with her, and wished to marry her. Accounts differ about what happened next: either Dwynwen said no because she was going to become a nun, or Brychan said no because he disliked Maelon and/or had arranged for Dwynwen to marry someone else. Consequently accounts also differ about the next step: either Maelon asked Dwynwen to elope with him, she said no, and he disappeared; or Maelon was so enraged by her rejection that he raped her, and then disappeared.

Either way, she prayed that she could forget Maelon, drank a potion an angel gave to her, and Maelon turned to ice. Dwynwen, upset about this, requested God to thaw him, to keep her from marrying ever, and to look kindly on true lovers, through Dwynwen herself. She thus became the patron saint of lovers. She then went to set up a convent on Ynys Llanddwyn, off Ynys Môn. She died around 460 AD.

If you look in shops where Welsh cards are sold, you will find them for Dydd Santes Dwynwen. Some restaurants are offering special menus on 25 January. But until we ask for more, Dwynwen will always be the poor relation of St Valentine!

 # Welsh Workshop

Dafydd:	Helo, Sally a Rob? Dych chi wedi cael 'Dolig neis?
Sally:	Neis iawn, diolch!
Rob:	Ie. Er … um … ymlaciol.
Mike:	A fi. Ac Anke.
Rob:	How do you know that?
Anka:	Ah – bore da, Howard! Blwyddyn newydd dda! Sut wyt ti y bore 'ma?

Howard:	Oh! Da iawn, diolch! A blwyddyn newydd dda i chi i gyd! Sut dych chi?
Dafydd:	Spesial, diolch!
Howard:	Ah – yn amlwg, dych chi'n dod o'r De!
Dafydd:	Yn amlwg – that means 'in the state of obvious', doesn't it? Is it OK to say 'spesial', then? It is something we say down south, as you say?
Howard:	Basically, rule of thumb is that if they say it where you live, adopt it! If I teach you the Welsh word for something, use it wherever possible, but if there's something like 'spesial' in the south, or 'champion' in the north, that's fine. It's in common usage.
Marian:	Yes, Geraint says 'champion' all the time.
Howard:	Right then. To work. We now need to look at the future tense of 'bod' – the 'will be' tense. Here on the board is the structure:

bydda i	I will be
byddi di	you will be
bydd e	he will be
bydd hi	she will be
bydd Huw	Huw will be
byddwch chi	you will be
byddwn ni	we will be
byddan nhw	they will be
bydd y dynion	the men will be

I also want to introduce a question-word to you – beth – 'what'. You can use 'beth' to say, for example, 'What are you doing?' (question) and 'I didn't know what you were doing' (statement). (Some question-words in Welsh have different forms for questions and statements.) For now, I want you to make up 10 sentences which use 'beth', and the future tense of 'bod'.

Your turn!
EXAMPLE: **Beth byddi di'n wneud heno?**
1.
2
3.
4.
5.
6.
7.
8.
9.
10.

 Coffee time

Anka: Howard, you've been talking to us about speaking Welsh to people, and having a go, but when people hear my Slovenian accent, they assume I can't speak Welsh, and speak to me in English! Is it rude then to speak Welsh to them?

Howard: Of course it's not rude! Any Welsh-speaker would be delighted. I certainly would be!

Mike: So what about starting a conversation with someone you don't know?

Howard: It's a sad fact that if a Welsh speaker opens up a dialogue with me, more often than not he or she will begin in English – because they don't know me. And even if they have a Welsh accent in English, that's not a guarantee that they speak Welsh. So, how do I get the conversation switched over to Welsh?

Dafydd: Yes, I was going to ask you that.

Howard: He might might say something in English like – 'These seagulls are a nuisance,' and I would come back with 'O, ia', or something similar that would make sense in both Welsh and English, but sounds more Welsh (in the north, at least!). Then they would switch to Welsh. So I haven't had to get into the (rather artificial) rigmarole of saying 'Dych chi'n siarad Cymraeg ?' ('Do you speak Welsh?') which I find a bit tiresome. If I was in Paris, I wouldn't ask someone 'Parlez-vous francais?' would I?!

Rob: Should we always try to start a conversation in Welsh, then?

Howard: My own personal principle is this – if I start a conversation, I always start it in Welsh. The other person might then say, 'I don't speak Welsh'. So then I will politely switch to English, but without apologising for speaking the Welsh. In this way, I am asserting the language and making sure that the person is aware that the language is alive.

Sally: Yes, my mother is amazed to find that the children speak nothing but Welsh at school. She thought the language had died long since.

Howard: It's surprising the number of visitors who think that Welsh is dying or nearly dead. I've even met people living within 40 miles of the border who didn't realise that we have our own language, even with Radio Cymru spilling over into large parts of England – I've picked it up on FM in Dorset and in London!

Marian: Yes, I have a friend in Somerset who watches Pobl y Cwm regularly!

Howard: Even while you are learning Welsh, and particularly when you are fluent, I strongly suggest that you always begin a conversation in Welsh – and then, if necessary, switch to English. And I ask all my Cymry Cymraeg friends this: "If you start a conversation with a stranger, please start it in Welsh". Starting in any other language just simply undermines the status of Welsh.

Learner of the Month:
Heather Jones

Heather Jones is one of the best-known singers of Welsh folk songs. Her most recent CD, 'Enaid', was released in November 2006.

'I was born in Cardiff, to parents who didn't speak Welsh. My great-grandfather, William Morris-Jones, kept a grocer's shop in Aberaeron, west Wales. His son (my father's father) had to leave the area in search of work. He and his four sisters all spoke Welsh, but he married a lady who didn't, so the language was lost.

'I loved learning Welsh in school. Our teacher inspired me to speak the language. I used to practise with my grandfather, out of earshot of Grandmother! I fell in love with Welsh folk songs, and when at eleven years old I found I could sing, I dedicated my whole life to singing in Welsh.

'I also had to improve my spoken Welsh, and went to classes at the Aelwyd (Youth Club) under the superb direction of teacher Gwilym Roberts. I was inspired by Dr Meredydd Evans, whose faith in me never faltered. He was then Head of Light Entertainment at the BBC, and gave me an audition when I was 16, and then my very own series, 'Gwrando ar Fy Nghân'

Photo: Raymond Daniel

(Listen to my Song)! I was able to choose my guests, and it was one of the first programmes to have an electric band on Welsh television. After that I did pantos, musicals, and many other things – all in Welsh. In 1974 I played the lead in the first-ever rock opera, 'Nia Ben Aur', in the Caernarfon Eisteddfod. In 1976 I started my own Welsh rock band; I also sang in a jazz band in London for a while – with Annie Lennox, before she was famous!

'By around 1980, I was back in Wales singing folk songs, and today – forty years on – I still continue to sing in Welsh. All my children, plus my granddaughter, speak Welsh. I am proud that I have brought the Welsh language back to the Morris-Joneses!'

Glossary

Calennig	New Year's presents	plentyn/plant	child/children
Yr Hen Galan	the old New Year	blwyddyn newydd dda!	Happy new year!
bore 'ma	this morning	yn amlwg	obviously
heno	tonight	ymlaciol	relaxing

Additional reading

There are many books in English, about Cymru, which will give you an interesting background to the current state of the nation. For example, look at books from the catalogues/websites of publishers Y Lolfa, Gomer, and the University of Wales Press. Here are two to start you off:

The Welsh Extremist Ned Thomas (Y Lolfa, £5.95)

A series of very readable essays, first published in the 1970s but still current in that they shed light on the current situation of the Welsh language. Ned questions and examines the use of the word 'extremist' as used by many for those of us who are prepared to fight for the right of the Welsh language to survive and prosper. He tells of the history of Cymdeithas yr Iaith Gymraeg (see p. 96, Tim Webb, one of the Learners of the Month); and of the Welsh Language Acts and how far they go… or not. And there are wonderful potted biographies of some of the most important writers in Welsh: Kate Roberts, Gwenallt, and Saunders Lewis.

History of Wales John Davies (Penguin, £16.99)

John Davies is one of the most eminent historians in Cymru. His comprehensive history of Cymru is described as 'relaxed, benign, witty, engaging', and so it is. It's the sort of book that gives you clues, and makes you want to discover more.

February/*Chwefror*

I think February was my 'Over the top, boys!' time. A rather public 'no going back' experience.

A friend and I decided to start a campaign group, '100 Ceredigion', against Ceredigion County Council's plan to build 6500 houses in the county. We called an inaugural meeting, and nine of us got together.

Eight Welshmen, and me.

Eight Cymry Cymraeg, and me.

And they knew I was a learner, but the new Chair of the group said, 'Jen, you can take notes.' Now, some might think that was just because I am a woman. However, I prefer, optimistically, to think it was to help my learning! Certainly, it did help.

My first response, however, was, 'Oh, come on! I can't do that! In Welsh? You have to be joking. One of you should do it.' But they told me to take the notes in English, and check things out with them. So off I went. A meeting of about 1½ hours. Northerners, Southerners, and a Cardi (I promise you, if you can understand Cardi-Welsh, you can understand anyone). The concentration involved was phenomenal. By the end of the evening I was exhausted.

But I'd done it! And when I checked out the notes, I found they were quite adequate!

It seemed unkind at first. It felt unkind. But I knew it wasn't meant that way. They were very encouraging and supportive. But my feelings of inadequacy in that and subsequent meetings were a tremendous incentive to keep improving. Those Cymry Cymraeg were dragging me (kicking and screaming!) out of my comfort zone.

That's part of the problem with learning Welsh in Wales. You can choose not to get into difficult situations, because everyone speaks English anyway.

So on the one hand, you can almost totally avoid embarrassment – but on the other, you can also avoid these life-changing events. I've heard far too many stories about non-Welsh-speaking people becoming members of committees of Welsh-speaking people, and the committee then switches to English. Not good enough! If this is your position, get them to continue in Welsh! Yes, it's hard, frustrating, demoralising, and DO be careful you understand what you're voting for. (I speak from personal experience here – a lesson learned the hard way!) But a) it undermines the status of the Welsh language if fewer and fewer things are done through Welsh, and b) it won't help your learning of Welsh.

Another good thing about attending Welsh-language meetings is that, even if you don't understand everything, you can pick up words. Listen for something that gets repeated, write down what it sounds like, ask someone later, or look it up. At one meeting I got the word 'tanseilio' (to undermine), and at another, 'er enghraifft' (for example). It doesn't have to be a total waste of your time! Open your mind a little!

And after the meeting, you can ask someone to tell you the main points. Believe me, they will be supportive (and if they're not, let me know!). They will (or should!) appreciate your keenness to learn, and to support, Welsh.

I have to confess that most of the Cymry Cymraeg I know are 100% supportive of people's efforts to learn the language, and their encouragement has been a tremendous help to me. Finding this sort of support, from Welsh-speaking family, friends, or colleagues, is invaluable. Their pleasure when you begin to use their language, however falteringly, is wonderful.

• Learning tip of the month

Take an A4 sheet of paper. Fold it into 4 from top to bottom, then across the middle. Open it out and then cut it into 8 pieces. Staple the top. You now have a tiny note-pad which will fit in a pocket or bag. Use it to 'collect' words. Words you hear and you work out the meaning; words you hear and which you want to look up later.

Of course, if you've learned pronunciation accurately, you can make an educated guess at the spelling, which will help you look up the word later!

14 February: St Valentine's Day – see January!

Website of the month

www.cyd.org.uk

Information, articles, competitions. There is an English-language option.

CYD is an organisation that links learners of Welsh with fluent speakers of the language – either first-language Welsh-speakers, or those who have learned to a reasonable level. There is a CYD magazine, and there are coffee mornings, walks, parties, and other activities, held totally in Welsh – but never fear! Those taking part are all either learners or else totally sympathetic with you as you struggle to improve! It's worth looking out for your local events, or if you have no access to the web, then phone the CYD office in Aberystwyth (01970 622143), and ask for more details.

'Book' of the month

If you want to know more about Cymru, from all sorts of perspectives, take out a subscription to *Cambria.*
It comes out bi-monthly, and is a nice glossy publication, and in English. You can learn a lot about Wales *while* learning Welsh! There are politics, culture, history, opinion, places to go, book reviews, and a feature for Welsh-language learners – just about everything, in fact!

Welsh Workshop

Howard:	Helo! Bore da! Ydych chi'n iawn y bore 'ma? Yn barod i weithio?
Mike:	Na. Mae pen tost 'da fi.
Anka:	Your own fault. I told you not to mix your drinks.
Rob:	Well, I feel great this morning. What is it … er … oh, yes, gwych! Hollol wych. There you are, mutating at 9.30 in the morning – can't be bad.
Howard:	[tongue in cheek] Gest ti beint o 'Uinness' neu ddau, Mike?
Sally:	Oh, nice – mutated Guinness. Like it.
Anka:	Peint o Uinness, ychydig o Fodca, Blydi Mary, ac ar ôl potel o win coch dros swper!
Mike:	Don't talk about it. I'm here, aren't I?
Howard:	[defnitely tongue in cheek!] Well, please don't do it again before a workshop! Guinness, Vodka, cocktail and a bottle of red – you're here to improve your Welsh, Mike!
Mike:	OK, OK, point taken.
Dafydd:	Well, at least we now know how to order a selection of drinks! What's beer, Howard?
Howard:	Lovely! Oh, sorry, cwrw! And you've got gwin gwyn – white wine – and you can order sych – dry, or canolig – medium, or melys – sweet.
Mike:	Coffi du i fi, plis. Strong. Very strong.
Anka:	Cryf iawn, Mike. Syniad da. A dŵr hefyd, dw i'n meddwl.
Howard:	Da iawn, Anka. Syniad da. Especially y dŵr – lots of it. That's water, Sally.
Sally:	Thanks – and 'syniad da'?
Howard:	Good idea.
Rob:	Syniad da, Anka. What's 'excellent idea', Howard?
Howard:	Syniad ardderchog! And a bad idea is a 'syniad gwael'. Like Mike's binge.
Mike:	Yeah, yeah. OK, let's get on with some Welsh now, shall we?
Dafydd:	Goodness! Well, if Mike wants to learn some Welsh, I reckon we should!
Howard:	Dw i'n cytuno! Agreed! And today we're going to look at ways of saying 'there is', and 'there are'. It's just a way of saying that something exists somewhere. For example, there is bread in the cupboard. Mae bara yn y cwpwrdd. You can ask questions by changing 'mae' to 'oes': 'Oes bara yn

y cwpwrdd?' (which means, 'Is there bread in the cupboard?') And the answer is – ?

Rob: Oes!

Howard: Da iawn, Rob! Rŵan ta, compare the following two sentences:

Mae'r llaeth yn y cwpwrdd.	The milk is in the cupboard.
Mae bara yn y cwpwrdd.	There is bread in the cupboard. (Literally, Bread is in the cupboard)

Now let's convert them to questions. All you do is kick out the 'mae' and put 'oes' in its place:

Oes car yn y garej?	Is there a car in the garage?
Oes tebot ar y bwrdd?	Is there a teapot on the table?

Right – so now, how do we answer these questions? Remember that we don't answer with 'yes' or 'no' as such, so the positive answer will be the equivalent of 'There is' – 'oes' – and the negative will be the equivalent of 'There isn't' – 'nac oes' (north) or 'nag oes' (south). Who's going to have a go?

Marian: Dafydd, oes car yn y garej?

Dafydd: Nag oes.

Rob: Mike, oes tebot ar y bwrdd?

Mike: Nac oes – yn anffodus!

Sally: Phew! Have we got any more time, Howard?

Howard: Beth?

Sally: Ah! Oes rhagor o amser 'da ni? Can I check up on names of months and stuff? I thought it was mis Chwefror now, but someone called it something else last week.

Howard: Mis Bach!

Mike: Must remember that. Very appropriate and reassuring. Nasty damp miserable month.

Anka: Dw i'n gwybod bod pen blwydd i ym mis Mawrth. Oh, er, sorry, fy mhen blwydd i!

Mike: Mis nesa, te. Hmm. Must remember that too!

Dafydd: Mae pen blwydd i ym mis Hydref. October.

Howard: Mis Medi ydw i, felly y mis cyn Dafydd.

Dafydd: Ond dim yr un oed, dw i'n siwr!

Howard: Dim cweit, dw i'n meddwl! Beth am Sally?

Sally: Ooh, er, mis Ebrill – yr un peth â Rob, fel mae'n digwydd!

Howard: Beth am y Nadolig?

Marian: Mis Rhagfyr. Y mis ar ôl mis Tachwedd.

Rob: Ac ar ôl hynny, mis Ionawr.

Howard: Felly: Ionawr, Chwefror, Mawrth, Ebrill – couple missing – ?

Sally: Mai? Mehefin?

Howard: Da iawn – ac wedyn – ?

Anka: Mis Gorffenaf?

Howard: Iawn – a beth am y Steddfod?

Marian: Mis Awst. Wedyn, mis Medi, mis Hydref, mis Tachwedd, a mis Rhagfyr. Ydw i'n iawn?

Howard: Da iawn!

Sally: I love the seasons of the year, they are really important to me. I know mis Hydref is October and hydref is the autumn – what are the others?

Howard: Spring is 'gwanwyn', Summer is 'haf', and Winter is 'gaeaf'. And by the way, don't forget that though the days don't mutate – dydd Llun, dydd Mawrth, etc – the nights do, so you have nos Lun, nos Fawrth, nos Fercher, and nos Wener.

Rob: Ydy'n bosibl gofyn rhywbeth arall?

Howard: Ydy, yn ystod amser coffi! Rŵan!

Mike: Howard, can I ask you to think about something for next month?

Howard: Easter eggs?

Mike: [laughs] No! Adjectives!

Howard: OK, next month, adjectives!

Coffee time

Mike: I've noticed something, Howard. Welsh plurals are tricky. I've been looking in this dictionary, and there are loads of ways of making plurals. English is much easier.

Howard: Hmm, well, I wouldn't say that. It's just what's most familiar to you. That doesn't mean it's the best language! Now, in English, the so-called 'standard' way of forming a plural is to add either an 's' or an 'es' to the word. But what is the determining factor? How would someone who is learning English as a foreign language tackle the matter? Is there a nice, tidy rule? Well, assuming the learner of English has sussed out the system, you might then think it's a doddle. Let's try a few sentences that the learner of English might produce:

There are five mans in that house.
I really hate mouses.
My tooths are hurting!

But, in English, 'man' becomes 'men' and not 'mans', 'mouse' becomes 'mice' and not 'mouses', and 'tooth' becomes 'teeth' and not 'tooths'. Let's have a shot at a few more:

The Beatles used to have millions of fen.
My brother owns two hice, and lives in the smaller one.
There are three phone beeth in this street.
Drat and double drat, as Dick Dastardly used to say.

Ain't as easy as it looks, is it ?

Mike: Er, no, put like that. So, how can we learn Welsh plurals?

Howard: When tackling Welsh plurals, similar situations crop up, but there are so many variations, that you can't really say that there is a regular plural formation (equivalent to the –s and –es situation in English). There are certain groups of words which seem to follow so-called conventions, but with lots of exceptions. A large number of Welsh nouns pluralise with 'au' on the end. There are so many way of forming plurals that, to be honest, I reckon it's easier just learning the plural forms as they come – learn the plural form of a word when you learn the singular. But in my view, swotting up on lists (in any language) is worse than being stuck in a lift with Radio 1 belting through the musak speakers! The other way of learning plural forms is to acquire them gradually by listening to as much Welsh as possible.

Mike: Oh. Not a lot of help available, then. It's just a case of trying to get it right and maybe sounding daft.

Howard: Welsh has one advantage over English – you use the singular form of the word straight after a number. So 'four cars' is 'pedwar car' and not 'pedwar ceir'. 'Three men' is 'tri dyn' and not 'tri dynion' and 'eight girls' is 'wyth merch'. A bit like English-speakers who talk about something measuring 'four foot' instead of 'four feet'. Mind you, there are other things to think about when using the number 2 in Welsh. To be discussed another day!

Un ddafad = one sheep
Dwy ddafad = two sheep
Mae'r defaid (plural sheep) yn sefyll yn y stryd.

Learner of the month: Jaci Taylor

'I had my first taste of learning Welsh when I attended an evening class in the village primary school where my eldest daughter was a pupil. I guess we received a note from the school asking us to come along to the Welsh class. I remember being absolutely petrified as I sat at the back of the classroom of some 20 people waiting for my turn to say what to me what was a totally incomprehensible sentence. Time passed with not much progress until I met my partner of 26 years, who was in no doubt that I would be fine with Welsh!

'I moved to Aberystwyth in 1980 and was immediately submerged in a torrent of morning, afternoon and evening classes and social events – to the point of amnesia! There was no let-up: one plateau after another was reached where I felt that I could not utter another Welsh syllable for as long as I lived. But I was strongly encouraged to battle on, and was amazed to find myself speaking Welsh on coming round from an operation in Bronglais Hospital!

'After two or three years, I became a Welsh tutor, which accelerated my learning curve. In 1982 my partner and I were recruited to help establish a Ceredigion branch of CYD, a society which helps Welsh learners to use their Welsh in the community. This meant a lot of activity, and I was elected as the secretary of the local CYD branch – which meant that I had to write minutes in Welsh! I must say it was very 'pidgin' Welsh at the beginning, but as they say 'needs must', and my use of the impersonal tense progressed fairly rapidly – thanks mainly to my partner who is an excellent Welsh tutor.

'I do think that learning another language which you can use in your daily life as easily and comfortably as your first language gives one a great sense of achievement – considering that I was an absolute dunce at French in school. The nuances of the language

– just hearing people speaking it, and then the music of Wales and its culture, so very different to my own background – a whole new world which I am now part of. I use Welsh every day, of course, at home and work. I worked for CYD for 10 years, where I spoke Welsh ninety percent of the time, whether working in the office, at branch meetings, or in meetings with the Welsh Language Board and other organisations who promote the use of the Welsh language. I now work as a development officer for the Mid-Wales Welsh for Adults Centre. I know that I have been very lucky to have been surrounded by Welsh speakers, whereas other people live in non-Welsh surroundings. But even so, it is possible to become fluent; there is a lot more provision for Welsh learners these days, especially on the internet. Crossing the bridge to fluency is just a stone's throw away.

Mae'r ci yn y lolfa (yn gwylio'r teledu!).

Glossary

gwael	poor, base, vile	**peint**	pint
hollol	absolutely	**cwpwrdd**	cupboard
fodca	Vodka	**bara**	bread
blydi	bloody	**garej**	garage
potel	bottle	**tebot**	teapot
dros	over	**yn anffodus**	unfortunately
swper	supper	**rhagor**	more
cwrw	beer	**amser**	time
gwin	wine	**gwanwyn**	Spring (the season)
gwyn	white	**gaeaf**	winter
sych	dry	**haf**	summer
canolig	medium	**hydref**	autumn
melys	sweet	**dyn/dynion**	man/men
du	black	**car/ceir**	car/cars
cryf	strong	**merch/merched**	girl/girls
syniad	idea	**cytuno**	to agree

March/Mawrth

March moved me forward again from the inaugural meetings of the campaign group '100 Ceredigion' to an interview on the television – S4C – in Welsh! A little contrived, shall we say, in that the interviewer wrote out on a card what he wanted me to say, and I read it in as natural a way as I could! A similar interview, in English, was broadcast on the BBC News, but I have no idea whether they ever used my Welsh bit on air. It wasn't the best Welsh-language interview they have ever done! But for me it was yet another step in the right direction.

The classes carried on towards Easter.

One good thing about classes is that you get lots of information about other courses. I discovered that in March there was a 'Sadwrn Siarad' in Aberystwyth. It's several hours of conversational Welsh, and exceptionally good value – I think I paid £3! I wandered in and found that I was with Julie, an excellent tutor, and two other students, one of whom was Gwyn, the keen guy from my class. As usual, I was the one with the confidence – that is, the one who talked too much – and they were the ones with the knowledge – that is, the ones who got things right! Oh to be both! They got grammar right, and mutations right, and remembered when to use 'yn', and that you don't use a plural noun straight after a number … all those basic things I'd not got hold of. I'd have stabs at things, much too quickly, and get lots wrong.

But by the end of the day I felt the benefit. It had been a 'stretching' day. But just as I'd experienced at the Nant almost a year before, by the end of it I was thinking in Welsh. Since the Nant, that day in Aberystwyth was the longest period of Welsh I'd had. And it worked.

Exposure like this is necessary for learners, and in many parts of Cymru there's not enough Cymraeg around, as an everyday occurrence. In Aberystwyth, my nearest town, it certainly isn't the first language most people speak when they go into shops. And neither is it the first language spoken by Welsh-speaking shop assistants, except in a couple of shops.

What I don't know is, how many people in shops, restaurants, etc in Aberystwyth speak English when they are at work, but are in fact Welsh-speakers I could address in Welsh! I have friends who address everyone in the Welsh language first. Why not? We live in Wales, after all! And a lot of people respond in Welsh. I tend to forget that most young people here have learned Welsh at school, at least from 11 to 14, and therefore can communicate in Welsh – even though they sometimes have to think a bit first! I'm a bit ashamed that in spite of my good intentions to start every conversation in Welsh, I fall short far too often. Must try harder!

Anyway, to get back to March 2003 – I also decided to enrol for a four-day course in April, just after Easter. The worrying thing was that it was called Cwrs Carlam – 'galloping course'! It sounded a bit too much like the Welsh Grand National for comfort!

Language tip

Someone told me a little 'rhyme':

1's a floozie,
2's a fly,
3, 4 and 6 are bly.

Doesn't make any sense, but it can help learners to remember the gender mutations for 1 year (un **flw**yddyn), 2 years (dwy **fly**nedd), and 3, 4 and 6 years (tair, pedair neu chwe **bly**nedd).

There are three numbers in Welsh that are gender-sensitive: 2, 3,and 4. So, for example, dau ddyn = two men, and dwy ddynes = two women. Thus dau is two masculine and dwy is two feminine. It's better to just learn the phrase 'dwy ferch' and store this in your brain than to learn the fact that 'dwy' is two feminine, then the fact that 'dynes' is feminine, and then the rule 'apply feminine versions of 2, 3, 4 to feminine entities'. Trying to apply rules as you speak can cause you to trip up. Just store 'dwy ddynes' and 'dwy ferch', etc, and retrieve these 'en bloc' as required.

Dydd Gŵyl Ddewi: St David's Day

March 1st is the natonal day of Wales. Dewi – St David – is our patron saint. It is known that he died in 589, but 1 March might have been the day of his death or of his birth; no-one is sure. Although his day isn't celebrated as fulsomely as the Irish celebrate St Patrick's Day, there are attempts to get it made a public holiday. Many schools have Eisteddfodau on that day, many people wear daffodils or leeks, and some people wear the national costume – well, the girls, especially in schools, wear what is traditionally seen as our national costume, and the boys wear red rugby shirts! My opinion is that every self-respecting Welsh company should close, and every self-respecting Welsh person should independently take a day off work, in order to prove that a national day would be welcome – but that's just my opinion!

You know that old myth about English tourists going into shops and finding people speaking English, and they then switch to Welsh so they can talk about the tourists without them understanding? Load of rubbish. It's partly a perception problem – a lot of Welsh-speakers use a lot of English words in their conversations. People walk into a shop and hear English words, and then hear Welsh, and jump to the wrong conclusions! In fact, Welsh people are far more likely to switch to English when someone comes in who doesn't speak Welsh – or simply carry on their own conversation in their own language. Let me tell you a story of something that happened recently that confirmed this to me.

I have a large plate I wanted to display. I went into a china shop in Aberystwyth to see if they had a stand for it. As I went in, there were two assistants sorting out a display, and talking with the woman behind the counter, in Welsh. Try as I might, though, I couldn't work out what 'plate stand' would be in Welsh, so I asked in English. The two women were still talking to each other in Welsh – until they heard me speaking English, when they immediately and automatically switched to English! Then I said, 'I would have asked for it in Welsh, but I didn't know what 'plate stand' was!' There followed a discussion in English, about 'plate stand', and they didn't know what it was either, but I said, in Welsh, 'Don't worry about it, I've got what I wanted now.'

The woman behind the counter looked at me with surprise. 'Oh, you speak Welsh.'

'Well, I'm learning.'

And the two women assistants started talking to each other in Welsh again, commenting to me that my Welsh was very good indeed.

Now, I understand why the woman behind the counter spoke English to me – I spoke English to her first, after all – but what about the others? Why did they speak English to each other? So as not to offend me? That is often the reason given for switching to English – they don't want to 'offend' people. But how many people ARE offended? Too many, that's for sure!, but HOW many? The sort of people who are offended when people speak Spanish in Spain, perhaps – but HOW many? Certainly never enough to justify turning from Welsh to English!

Book of the month

Welsh Roots and Branches: Gwreiddiadur Cymraeg
Gareth Jones (Tre Graig Press, £15.00)

Gareth Jones had the idea for this book after trying to read Welsh, with the help of a dictionary. The realisation about the way the language is built up helped him learn Welsh, and now he has produced this book. It's a fascinating book of lists, of connections, and of enlightenment. If you enjoy words, you'll enjoy this.

Website of the month

www.aber.ac.uk

The University of Wales has set up an on-line dictionary of the Welsh language. It is still being developed, but it shows promise!

Welsh Workshop

Howard: Bore da. Sut ydych chi i gyd heddiw?

Marian: Iawn, diolch, Howard – and er – especially …?

Howard: Yn enwedig.

Marian: Ac enwedig oherwydd y sgwrs ar y ffôn 'da ffrind neithiwr – yn y Gymraeg!

Rob: What was that all about, then?

Marian: Dim byd cyffrous. Only the words all of you here know!

Howard: Wel, da iawn. Unrhyw un arall wedi cael sgwrs yn y Gymraeg?

Dafydd: Unrhyw un arall – oh, anyone else! Fi. Gyda'r boi yn y Cwps yn Aberystwyth. Roedden ni'n siarad am y griced ar y teledu.

Mike: Do'n i ddim yn gwybod ti'n hoffi criced, Dafydd.

Dafydd: Dw i ddim! Dim o gwbl! Ond dywedodd y boi 'na bod e'n gêm ffantastig. Anhygoel.

Rob: Anhygoel …?

Howard: Unbelievable! Yn cytuno, Dafydd. Gêm araf a ddiflas iawn iawn.

Sally: Wel, dw i ddim yn cytuno! Dw i wedi hoffi criced ers o'n i'n ifanc. Gêm o dactics ydy hi. Rhy anodd i chi ei ddeall, efallai.

Mike: Cytuno, Sally! Anarferol ffeindio ferch sy'n hoffi criced.

Anka: Criced?

Mike: I'll explain over supper. It'll take some time …

Howard: Ond – gwych clywed chi'n siarad y Gymraeg! Yn amlwg, 'dych chi wedi bod yn gweithio'n galed ers y cyfarfod diwetha – yn eich dosbarthiadau, a tu allan hefyd. Well done – it's not enough to leave everything to your tutor. Working outside the dosbarth is absolutely key to your progress. Llongyfarchiadau! Rŵan 'ta. Heddiw: dw i eisiau siarad am ansoddeiriau. Ansoddeiriau – ?

Marian: Adjectives?

Howard: Iawn. Sut i gymharu pethau a phobl. Iawn? Pawb yn deall?

Rob: This is going to be tricky. I wouldn't know an adjective if I saw one in English, let alone in Welsh. Can you give me a few examples, Howard, please?

Howard: Ah. An adjective is a word that describes something or someone – like:

big, little, tall, short, wet, dry. Here are some more examples.

big	little	tall	short	wet	dry	thin
mawr	**bach**	**tal**	**byr**	**gwlyb**	**sych**	**tenau**

Rob: Felly: sut wyt ti'n disgrifio dy hunan, Rob?
Disgrifio – to describe? Iawn. Wel, dw i'n dal, a thenau, dim lot o wallt, a llygaid glas.

Howard: Iawn. Wel, mae 'tal' yn ansoddair. A 'tenau' hefyd. A beth am Sally?

Rob: Ah. Rhaid i mi fod yn ofalus yma!

Sally: Too right.

Rob: Mae hi'n … erm … Dydy hi ddim yn dal iawn. Mae gwallt brown gyda hi (ond allan o botel – sori, Sally!) a llygaid gwyrdd.

Howard: Da iawn, Rob! Gwych. Ydy Sally yn dalach na ti, neu yn fyrrach?

Rob: O, mae hi'n fyrrach.

Howard: Iawn! The 'ach' is equivalent to '-er' in English, but like in English it's used on the end of shorter words. Sally, beth am Rob? Dyweda rywbeth amdano fo.

Sally: Wel, mae Rob yn dalach na fi.

Howard: Da iawn!

Dafydd: I've just realised. We've been speaking a huge amount of Welsh this session! Perhaps we're catching on!

Marian: Yes, I realised that, too. Great! Sori, gwych!

Howard: Mae'n digwydd fel 'na. You work and work and work and you think it'll never 'happen', that you'll never be able to speak Welsh, and then one day, bang! It works! Da iawn, pawb.

Anka: Yes, I've learned that. It's always worth carrying on even when you feel stupid, because it really will 'happen' one day. All this learning isn't wasted!

Rob: Yes, when I started I didn't really think I'd be saying things in Welsh fairly confidently. I'm really excited!

Howard: Right, well, let's capitalise on that enthusiasm! What about 'good, better, best' – 'da, gwell, gorau'? Let's do cwrw v. seidr v. lager. Rob, if you wanted to say that beer was better than cider, how would you?

Rob: Mae cwrw yn well na seidr.

Howard: Da iawn. 'Better than' = 'yn well na'.

Mike: Hold on – mae lager yn well na cwrw!

Marian: Na. Mae dŵr yn well na cwrw, seidr a lager!

Howard: Hey! Dim rhyfel yma! Iawn. Beth am goffi a te, Marian?

Marian: Erm … mae te yn well na coffi.

Howard: Dafydd?

Dafydd: Dw i'n hoffi coffi, ond ar ôl cael pysgod a sglodion, te ydy'r gorau.

Howard: Ardderchog, Dafydd, a dw i'n cytuno! I'll repeat it: te ydy'r gorau. Tea is best. Or even, tea is the best. Now, write sentences comparing the following sets of items:

Rolls-Royce	Ford Focus	Lada
Pizza	Fish and chips	Burgers
Gardening	Fishing	Playing golf

Coffee time

Rob: Ah. Howard. Right. I have a big problem. That is, gender.

Sally: Interesting – I hadn't noticed it being a problem!

Rob: Ha ha. Very funny. No, I mean in Welsh. We don't have gender problems in English.

Mike: No, English is much better. Sorry, different.

Howard: Right. Diolch, Anka, coffi du, cryf iawn, os gweli di'n dda!

Marian: Cryf *iawn*, Howard?

Howard: Yeah, I need it to cope with questions like this! Right. We usually attribute gender to living things – male or female. In many languages, the concept of gender flourishes and it reaches beyond biological life to inanimate objects as well. Linguists call this 'grammatical gender'. So, a chair could be masculine or feminine. In Welsh, it's feminine.

Dafydd: Can we know the weather is feminine, or chairs?

Rob: Well, the weather is obviously feminine! You never know what it's going to do next!

Marian: We'd bore you if we were predictable! So yes, you know weather is

Howard: feminine. But I take the point about chairs.

Howard: We can't work it out, no. We need to learn it. But it isn't a crime to get the gender wrong. Many languages have three 'genders' – masculine, feminine and neuter. German is an example of this.

Anka: Coffi, Howard.

Howard: Diolch! So, English and German, for example, have 'he', 'she', and 'it'. However, many languages, including French and Welsh, have only two – masculine and feminine – no separate 'it'. What deprivation!

Mike: Typical of Welsh to complicate matters. How do we cope with inanimate thingies, then?

Howard: In Welsh we attribute a 'he' or a 'she' to the inanimate. So, in French, for example, the weather is treated as masculine, and 'Il pleut' looks to the learner of French like 'He is raining' – literally, 'he rains'. But in Welsh, the weather is treated as feminine – 'Mae hi'n bwrw glaw' – 'She is raining'.

Mike: Looks tricky to me.

Howard: Well, it's easy, of course, if you are raised to speak a two-gender language as your mother tongue. Like most other features of the language, you just don't question the thing at all. But if you speak a three-gender language as your mother tongue, and then you start learning a two-gender language, you could find that this poses a problem. But it's like lots of other things – it will become second nature after a time.

Mae'r ferch yma yn canu mewn Eisteddfod Gŵyl Dewi Sant yn yr ysgol.

Learner of the month: Nigel Callaghan

'I started going to Welsh classes when I lived in Peterborough in the late 1980s. For some reason I had always wanted to learn: I think it was mainly because of my late grandfather, Taliesin Mordecai, who was a Welsh-speaker from Glamorgan. From Peterborough I attended various summer schools in Wales, and then moved to Wales in 1993. For a while I had to commute to a job in England, but eventually set up my own IT consultancy business in Ceredigion in 2002.

'That was when I was able to make the big step to becoming a Welsh speaker rather than a Welsh learner. Prior to that, Welsh was still something I wrote, studied, and used occasionally, rather than a living day-to-day language. Over the last few years Welsh has truly become a second language for me, which I use daily in a wide range of social and business situations. I am a self-employed IT consultant, specialising in bilingual website design. I deal with many of my clients entirely through the medium of Welsh, which includes discussions on extremely technical topics – Welsh is not just a language for the hearth and chapel!

'With the explosive growth of the Internet as a source of information and a medium for communication, it is essential that Welsh has its place there. I specialise in setting up websites in Welsh, as well as ensuring that the tools to build and manage those sites are available in Welsh as well. The growing availability of software both in Welsh (browsers, word processors etc) and to assist the writing of Welsh (spelling and grammar checkers) are important steps to creating an electronic Welsh-speaking Wales on the Internet.

'For me Welsh has also become a social and community language: several years ago I was invited to fill a vacancy on the Community Council. I was re-elected in 2004 and am currently serving as Chairman: the business of the Council is done entirely through Welsh (although translation facilities are provided). This was an important step for me in getting to know more of my neighbours and to becoming more integrated in the community. It is always difficult for newcomers to become part of an established community – if they cannot speak the first language of many members of that community it will be doubly hard. I have had an interest in local history for many years (and developed a bilingual website on the history of the parish) and it was a great honour when I was asked to address the village cultural society on my work on that website – through the medium of Welsh, of course!

There are so many other areas where Welsh has helped me meet new people – through Plaid Cymru, choirs, general community activities, and much more. It struck me recently how many people I now know in the area who I have never spoken English to. For me, the key was realising that you don't need to be perfect to use the language effectively, and developing the confidence to start a conversation with a stranger in Welsh, and to answer the phone in Welsh!'

Glossary

tenau	thin	**yn enwedig**	especially
oherwydd	because	**gwallt**	hair
sgwrs	conversation	**llygad/llygaid**	eye/eyes
ffrind	friend	**yn ofalus**	careful
neithiwr	last night	**melyn**	yellow
cyffrous	exciting	**gwyrdd**	green
teledu	television	**gwell**	better
anhygoel	unbelievable	**gorau**	best
diflas	miserable/boring	**seidr**	cider
ifanc	young	**sglodion**	chips
anodd	difficult	**byr**	short
ansoddeiriau	adjectives	**gwlyb**	wet
bach	small	**carlamu**	to gallop
tal	tall	**deall**	to understand

April/*Ebrill*

Ioan Guile, our Cymro Cymraeg tutor for the Cwrs Carlam, is famous in Aberystwyth. A lot of people simply call him 'Widow Twanky'! This is because, in another existence, Ioan plays the pantomime dame in the annual pantomime by the Aberystwyth Players. This I was told as we followed him up the path to our classroom in the University.

Ioan is wonderful. The life and soul. Funny, kind, astute, and knowledgeable. He knows that intensive courses can drain learners, and divides up the day into revision (first thing in the morning – thank you, Ioan, from a non-morning-person!), new stuff after the break, consolidation of new stuff after lunch, and then fun and games from 3.30 to 5pm. Including silly songs! Ioan is a good class-uniter – I would think all groups 'gel' with him as tutor. His warmth relaxes people quickly. We learnt fast.

I'm not generally in favour of 'go-rounds': 'Tell us all why you're here and what you want from the course,' but in a language class it's a good idea. You do it in the language you're learning, and the tutor gets some idea of what he's 'up against' in terms of who's at which level, and what sort of things need revising. Essential. An experienced tutor will be listening carefully to what you are saying about yourself, and beginning to get to know his learners as individuals. At the same time, in his head he is pulling out files of exercises and vocabulary, and putting some away, making a pile of things he thinks the class can cope with in the four days, and another pile of things that will stretch the higher-level people without consigning the lower ones to a pit of despair.

One thing we loved about Ioan was that he doesn't stop working at 5pm. If someone asked him a question he couldn't immediately answer, he would turn up the next morning with an answer, having pored over his books during the evening. Educational research has shown that if students like their teacher, they do better in that subject. This works for adults too! The feeling

was that if he was prepared to work hard for us, we would willingly work hard for Ioan. (The same has applied, for me, with Howard, Val, and various other tutors. Confession: I am afraid that a tutor who is rigid, judgemental, and non-warm brings out the rebel in me and prevents me learning, unless I 'get a grip'!)

We were talking in Welsh all through lunch and coffee breaks, and those who were residential on Cwrs Carlam were using the language all evening. The improvement was obvious. Some of my classmates, like me, didn't live or work with Welsh-speakers, but they improved fast. In just four days!

Cwrs Carlam convinced me once again that speaking Welsh was possible for me. By the end of the four days – well, by the end of Thursday, in fact – I couldn't think or speak in English at all! Only in Welsh. What a glorious feeling! It wore off a bit after a while, but I knew it was going to be possible for me to use 'the language of heaven' all the time, in time, if I needed to. I felt incredibly excited. Fired up.

Classes the week after that felt totally different. Yes, I needed the grammar bits of the Wlpan course, still, but I just wanted to chatter away in Welsh! My confidence had soared.

Try it! It cost so little, and it's such a short time. Give yourself a chance to live in a Welsh-speaking environment for just four days, and see what you gain. A lot of us were amazed. Perhaps you will be too!

 Book of the month

The Pocket Modern Welsh Dictionary (Oxford University Press, £9.99)

A dictionary that can become a 'book at bedtime' – readable, full of information, and indispensable. Nothing more to say!

Website of the month

www.clwbmalucachu.co.uk

Although some people don't like the title of this site (it means something like 'grinding shit'), many people enjoy the site itself. It helps you find CDs, courses and teachers, and there are short stories to read – some very short! – at various levels of Welsh. There is also a chat room where you can practise your Welsh.

Ti/chi: a dilemma for learners

In classes, when I started learning, I was told: 'Use 'ti' for people you know very well, animals, and children, and 'chi' for people you don't know very well, or for more than one.'

But in fact, it's not a straightforward concept, and if you haven't been brought up with the system it can be very confusing. (I've heard that only English and Hebrew don't have it – please correct me if I'm wrong!)

When I started getting to know Welsh-speakers, I discovered that it is much more individual than that!

One friend, who is in her seventies, told me that she calls everyone 'chi' if they are not in her family. So, I realised, even if I went to her house every day, and got to know her very well, she would never call me 'ti'. She calls her best friends 'chi'. (Some people call their parents 'chi'.)

Another friend knew me well for 18 months before suddenly changing to 'ti'. I have no idea what I'd done to deserve it! We'd discussed it earlier, and he explained the social problems that could come with calling someone 'ti' in public, especially someone of the opposite sex!

Another wrote to me to say that when we met next, she would begin to 'ti' me, and I have met some people who have called me 'ti' from the start. I'm not altogether happy with that, but realise it can be a compliment, a sort of acceptance.

I also met some A-Level students who were taught by their tutor 'not to bother with 'chi' except for plurals, because it's too posh'. Personally, I think that is a disgrace, because 'ti' and 'chi' is a wonderful system and a very important part of Welsh life and culture.

I made a bad mistake once after feeling that I knew someone quite well, and changing to 'ti' – only to be met with an embarrassed silence! Oops – I'd got it wrong! So I decided on a policy, and that is, not to change 'chi' to 'ti' myself, but to wait for the Welsh-speaker to change it. After all, it's not my native culture. It's lovely when someone changes to 'ti'. Thereafter, of course, for the learner it's a case of changing the grammar, and I still have a problem if I'm with two people, one a 'chi' and one a 'ti'! But I regard it as part of the beauty of speaking Welsh and having Welsh-speaking friends.

So, to summarise, it's a lot more socially acceptable to remain on 'chi' terms until the Cymry Cymraeg themselves change you to 'ti', and also, it removes from you the need to make the decision when to change.

Welsh Workshop

Mike: Ooh, that makes a change, we're first!

Anka: Yes, staying nearby on Friday night certainly makes a change.

Mike: Careful, don't broadcast the fact! We don't want it to be public just yet, do we.

Anka: I think Sally and Marian have guessed already.

Mike: Yeah, but Rob, Dafydd and Howard haven't. Let's keep it that way! Oh, hello, there, Dafydd! Sut mae?

Dafydd: Popeth yn iawn, diolch! Sut ydych chi'ch dau?

Anka: Iawn, diolch. Ydych chi'n iawn y bore 'ma, Mike?

Mike: Oh, helo, Anka – iawn, diolch! Bore da, Howard! O, a Sally a Rob! Bore da!

Howard: Bore da! Mae'n flin 'da fi mod i'n hwyr. Llawer o draffig. Let's get started. Reit 'ta, bawb, 'dyn ni'n mynd i edrych ar 'bod clauses' heddiw. We've seen that 'bod' is the verb 'to be', but it is also used in a particular way that you might not expect.

Rob: Thanks, Howard. I wish I knew more about English grammar, I'm sure it would help with Welsh grammar.

Howard: Well, yes and no. There are similarities, of course, but some differences, and many different terms. None of us explicitly learns the grammar of our first language, anyway, so don't feel bad. You just picked it up when you were a kid, didn't you. Your Mum didn't say, 'Now, Rob, when you said, 'Want chocolate', you didn't use a verb, or a subject,' did she. Well, I hope she didn't!

Rob: I can't imagine she did! Thank you, that's comforting. I was thinking I was stupid.

Sally: Well, you're not. But no, we don't say things like that to our kids. They just sort-of pick up their mother tongue. I wish it was the same with us learning Welsh.

Howard: It can be the same for adults too. You don't just have to 'learn' Welsh – you can 'pick it up' too! Think about it: you're living in a giant classroom! Welsh is everywhere! Choose to go to places where you hear Welsh. You'll hear it, and if you listen carefully, you'll also acquire it. You don't have to keep it in two-hour class-length doses! You hear Welsh when you pick up the kids from school, don't you. Keep listening!

Marian: But Geraint is worried that I'll pick up bad Welsh from him.

Howard: What does that matter? It'll be Welsh! And it'll be much more real than 'dosbarth-Welsh'. Just pick it up! From anywhere! And don't worry about being perfect. When kids learn their mother tongue, they aren't perfect at it, but it improves. You will too. Anyway – to work. What I want to look at is the use of 'bod' where you're saying things like 'I think that Siân is in Aberystwyth.' In English, you can say it that way, or 'I think Siân is in Aberystwyth', without the 'that'. Yn y Gymraeg: 'Mae Siân yn Aberystwyth'. But in Welsh it isn't quite right to say, 'Dw i'n meddwl mae Siân yn Aberystwyth.'

Marian: Hmm – well, how do we say it, then?

Howard: Have you ever heard people from some areas of England say, 'I think he be in the pub'? Well, I think that this is the case here. And that's how we use 'bod'– the verb to be – here. We need to change 'mae' to 'bod', so we have 'Dw i'n meddwl bod Siân yn Aberystwyth'. In effect, 'Mae Siân' = Siân is, and 'bod Siân' = Siân be. So we're actually saying, in Welsh, 'I think Siân be in Aberystwyth (ahar, Jim lad!).

Rob: Ah – I think I'm getting it – how about 'Dw i'n meddwl bod y car yn y garej'?

Howard: Da iawn, Rob! Exactly it. So, let's get you working, then! Translate the following sentences!

Your turn!	
I think that Twm is ill.	
I think the cheese is very good.	
Sioned thinks beer is better than cider.	
Gwilym thinks that Teifion is taller than Seimon.	

Howard: This 'bod' construction works with some other verbs too, for example, 'credu' – 'to believe'. And remember that in English you can say 'I believe that John is on holiday', which matches the Welsh perfectly.

Dafydd: I'm sure I've seen some books that say that 'bod' is equivalent to 'that' in this construction.

Howard: But I believe that's not the case. Using 'bod' as in 'I believe John be on holiday' makes perfect sense. In spoken English, the 'that' is optional – you can say I think John is working' or 'I think that John is working'. In this particular construction in Welsh, there is no 'that' at all. Now: try translating these:

I believe John to be very kind.	
They say that the weather is better in Ynys Môn.	
Mr Jones feels that the work is difficult.	
I hope the car is OK.	

 # Coffee time

Sally:	Howard, can you tell us a bit more about mutations? We've done things – the nasal one, isn't it – like 'ym Mangor', and 'fy nghar i', but what about the others? They scare me!
Howard:	Mutations aren't worth getting scared over, Sally. They're simply unfamiliar, that's all. They'll come in time. Let's talk about the aspirate mutation, which makes t into th, c into ch, p into ph. Think of 'TCP' and you'll remember it. It occurs in a number of contexts, for example, after 'ei' when 'ei' means *her* (possessive). In Welsh, the full form of the possessives – *my, your, his, her, our, your* (pl,) *their* – consist of two bits – one *either side* of the thing being possessed.
Rob:	Oo-er. It's going to take me a while to catch on to this.
Howard:	Yes, but you don't have to remember it all today! Just relax! Now, in the case of *her*, it goes like this: 'Her car' is *ei char (hi)*. 'Her head' is *ei phen (hi)*. 'Her house' is *ei thŷ (hi)*. In everyday Welsh, the *ei* is mostly pronounced '*ee*'. I've put brackets around the *hi* because it is often omitted in fast Welsh, and it is almost always omitted in posh literary Welsh. It can be used as emphasis: ei char *hi* = *her* car (i.e. it wasn't mine!).
Mike:	Oh, yes, I've heard that. Like, 'It was *your* fault.' I hear that often, in fact!
Howard:	You have to use the aspirate mutation quite strictly, because getting the mutation 'wrong' after *ei* could give rise to gender confusion especially if the *hi* is omitted. For example, if someone says 'ei car', it's not clear whether it means *his car* or *her car*, because *ei* can mean either! The context *might* resolve this but there's no guarantee. But don't get too worried about this. Listening as much as possible will embed it into your subconscious.
Rob:	Oh yeah?
Anka:	It will, Rob, it's the same with any language. Things seem difficult to

grasp at first, but the more we use them, the more they suddenly seem to be graspable.

Howard: Anka's quite right, and she speaks hundreds of languages, so she knows everything!

Anka: Not hundreds, quite! In our history we've had to learn several, depending on who was in control of our country. It's the same here, the English have been in control for centuries …

Howard: Er, yes, but we digress! Another context where the aspirate is used is after certain vowel sounds, usually *a* or *â*. 'a' can mean *and*, like in 'Pwllheli a Chaernarfon' or even 'Caernarfon a Phwllheli'.

Mike: Ah – no need to bother with them, then!

Howard: There is if you want to speak good Welsh, Mike, which of course you do! But Anka's right, think of mutations as a long-term acquisition process and not as a barrier to your progress, and you'll be absolutely fine. Welsh-speakers won't hassle you if you get them wrong – and if they do, report them to me, and I'll explain the process of learning a language!

Glossary

tŷ	house		llawer	a lot
pen	head		meddwl	to think

Wales doesn't have a monopoly on dragons! This is the Dragon Bridge, in Anka's home town, Ljubljana, in Slovenia.

Learner of the month: Phyllis Kinney

Phyllis lives in Cwmystwyth, Ceredigion. She is reputed to be in her 80s, though it's difficult to believe! Phyllis is an acknowledged expert on Welsh folk music, and writes books on the subject with her husband, Dr Meredydd Evans.

'I began to learn Welsh about 50 years ago. Most Welsh people I knew took pity on me as a struggling learner and spoke English to me, feeling it would be impolite not to do so. I found it easier to read Welsh, where I could take my time over the words. After going on an intensive crash course, my world changed. It was as if I had gone through an invisible curtain. My relationship with Welsh friends changed when they were able to speak their first language with me. I didn't stop being an American – I'll be that until I die – but I stopped looking from the outside in.

'Was it difficult? Yes, of course, but no harder than learning German. The pronunciation is easy – much easier than English, which seems to have no rules at all. Welsh is a phonetic language and once the values of each vowel and consonant have been learned it is possible to read a paragraph of Welsh with correct pronunciation, even if you don't understand the words!

'The best way, of course, is to do what I did – marry a Welsh speaker and make sure he talks Welsh to you. If that's not feasible, find a friend who is willing to speak Welsh to you even if your replies are usually in broken Welsh. Listen to Welsh radio programmes, read books and newspapers, and try to hear the language as much as possible. Gradually the unfamiliar mutations and the back-to-front word order will become natural and you will have joined a very select group – successful Welsh learners. Go for it! Good luck!'

May/Mai

I couldn't believe how much easier things were after Cwrs Carlàm. How could four days make so much difference? Using Welsh from 9-5 each day, including at breaktimes, had made me think in Welsh, and it changed everything. My twice-weekly Wlpan classes were easier. The correspondence course seemed much easier. Everything I did in Welsh was simply more natural.

I needed the email address of someone who owned a shop. I knew the staff in the shop spoke Welsh. So I took a deep breath, went in, and asked – in Welsh – whether Gerallt had an email address. The guy behind the counter said, in Welsh, 'Yes, of course,' and wrote it down for me. I thanked him, and left the shop. Only then did I remember to breathe out! I had done it, all in Welsh – without saying, as I usually did (to apologise for my bad Welsh, I guess), 'I'm learning Welsh'. In a sense it was an odd thing, and a small thing, to feel pleased about, but I did.

Then I went into the National Library and asked the woman at reception for my password. And I got it! I stood looking at it, thinking, 'No, this must be wrong, it can't possibly be that she understood me.' And I actually (shame, shame!) said, 'Excuse me, but this **is** my password, is it? Only I just wanted to know you understood what I'd asked for, because I'm only a learner of Welsh.'

And she smiled very kindly, and said, 'Yes, it is, and your Welsh is fine, don't worry!'

It felt like only a few weeks away from my Challenge deadline, 1 September. My anxiety that I wouldn't beat The Challenge pushed me on. I read as much Welsh as possible. I began to buy *Golwg* ('a look', 'view', 'appearance') – a weekly news magazine. Reading it was very hard work, but at least I could see what was 'news' in the Welsh-speaking world, even if I couldn't understand all of what was said.

 Book of the month

There is a saying, 'If you're not confused, you're not learning'. Yes, if you think about it, between the 'I don't know' stage and the 'I know' stage of learning anything, there is a natural stage, 'I'm confused'. Therefore, if you **are** confused, you **are** learning. You're stepping from 'I don't know' towards 'I know'. Expect to be confused. It's **natural**. And since moving forward is what it's all about, the 'being confused' stage is also essential. Don't mix up 'being confused' with 'being stupid'! You may **feel** stupid, but just carry on. Remember that all fogs clear with time!

And I decided then that in order to be completely ready for 1 September, I would enrol for a four-week intensive Welsh course in Aberystwyth during August. Surely that would iron out a lot of faults in my Welsh and get me thinking in Welsh in time for my 'exam' on 1 September! If I didn't die of exhaustion first …

Book of the month

***Enwau Cymraeg i Blant/Welsh Names for Children* Heini Gruffudd (Y Lolfa, £3.95)**

When I moved to Cymru, I was quite surprised to come across people with unfamiliar names. Some I'd seen before, like Dafydd, or Dai, or Huw; others were very unfamiliar, like Gerallt. It was a delight to discover this. As the author says on the back cover, 'It's a key to the many treasures of Wales'.

And while we're on the subject of names, many people I know have 'Welshified' their names, overturning the Anglicisation that had happened through the centuries. (Heini Gruffudd is one of them, as it happens.) And there are far too many 'Joneses' – another Anglicisation that has spurred some people to drop the 'Jones' and use just their first names – people like Dafydd Iwan (now a business man, but also an extremely influential singer), and Alun Ffred (politician) – two 'Jones' brothers. I have myself changed from 'Lewis', an Anglicisation of 'Llywelyn'. And the very same thing should happen to house names! – and there's a website about them, too.

Below you will see some of the Welsh personal names used in this book, and the meanings of the names as taken from Heini Gruffudd's book.

Idris	from Cader Idris	**Melangell**	daughter of Tudwal ap Ceredig
Ieuan	from the Latin Ioannes, a form of John	**Nia**	in Irish legend, Nia went with Osian to Tir-na n-og, land of youth
Steffan	from Greek 'crown'.	**Catrin**	from Greek, then Latin, 'pure'
Dylan	son of Aranrhod. Sea god, or hero of fables	**Sioned**	Diminutive of Siân or fem. of Sion
Meredydd	a great lord	**Glenys**	glân = clean, fair, holy
Geraint	from Greek, 'old'	**Siân**	feminine version of Sion, a form of 'Ioan'
Dafydd	from Hebrew, 'darling', then 'friend'.	**Llywelyn**	llyw = leader; eilyn = likeness (?)
Heini	sprightly, active; a soldier who went to Catraeth	**Mererid**	precious stone
Huw	Old German 'Hugi' = 'mind, heart'	**Mair**	from Hebrew, 'a wished-for child'. Biblical = Mary

Customs: May: Calan Mai (1st of May)

Long before 'Labour Day', May Day was celebrated in many parts of Wales. Sometimes a maypole was used, sometimes not. There was much dancing and feasting. It sounds much more fun than Bank Holiday Monday!

 ## Website of the month

www.madog.org

This is the website for Cymdeithas Madog. The Welsh Studies Institute in North America Inc. is a tax-exempt, non-profit organization dedicated to helping North Americans learn, use and enjoy the Welsh language. It takes its name from Madog ab Owain Gwynedd, a Welsh prince who sailed (according to legend) to America in the 12th century. That makes him a fitting symbol of the cultural and linguistic links which Cymdeithas Madog maintains between Wales and the New World.

It's interesting to see how international Welsh is, and the sort of activities that the American Welsh-language learners get up to! There is stuff here for learners, and all kinds of news.

Dw i'n meddwl bod hynny'n ddigon o laeth am heddiw!

Welsh Workshop

Howard: Wel, bore da, bawb, a chroeso i'r gweithdy olaf ond un – your penultimate workshop!

Mike: Ahh. Next one will be the last. Sad.

Dafydd: These workshops have been really useful alongside our normal classes. Well, I think so, anyway.

Sally: They've certainly helped me. I've realised I've been learning far more than I thought, in the classes and outside them.

Rob: Yes, even I've found them helpful!

Mike: I hate to say it, but I've even begun to enjoy Welsh! I was finding the classes a bit dry, but with the workshops as well, and meeting all of you, I've found other incentives to learn.

Dafydd: Well, that's a refreshing change!

Howard: Reit. Rŵan 'ta, heddiw 'dyn ni'n mynd i edrych ar y ferf 'cael'. Be' ydy 'cael' yn Saesneg?

Marian: Er – to have. Ond, mae e'n dweud yma yn y Geiriadur Mawr, 'To have, to get, to obtain, to gain, to win, to find.' And it says, 'Cael a chael' is 'touch and go', and 'ar gael' is 'to be had'.

Howard: Yeah, that's 'to be had' as in 'available', not 'to be had' as in 'I've been had'! But yes, a number of related meanings. It can also mean 'to have permission, and it has a passive meaning which I'll tell you about as well.

Dafydd: Waw! We're going to learn a lot this morning!

Howard: Rŵan 'ta, 'cael'. The basic present tense construction is like all the others: 'Dw i'n cael brecwast am 8 o'r gloch yfory.' I'm having breakfast at 8 o'clock tomorrow. But it can also work with habitual things: 'Dw i'n cael brecwast am 8 o'r gloch y bore' – I have breakfast at 8 o'clock every morning. Here, 'cael' conveys 'have' in the sense of 'consume'.

Anka: Can it be used with something we're not actually consuming? Like fun? Can we say, 'Dw i'n cael hwyl' for 'I am having fun'?

Howard: Yep, that works too. And 'cael' can also convey 'to get', or 'to obtain' – for example, 'Dw i'n mynd i gael y papur' – 'I'm going to get the paper'. Can you think of when it is not used?

Dafydd: I would think, not in sentences like 'I have a car' in the sense of 'I possess a car'.

Howard: Right. Anyone else?

Sally: I don't think it's used in the case of 'I have to go now', in the sense of 'must' – that's 'rhaid'; or in the sense of 'I have seen the film' – that's 'wedi', isn't it.

Howard: Da iawn, Sally. An interesting use of 'cael' is in the sense of 'being allowed to' – e.g. 'Dych chi ddim yn cael parcio yn y Stryd Fawr' – 'You are not allowed to park in the High Street'.

Rob: What about ordering things? Asking for things? Like in a caffi? 'Can I have soup', for instance? Do you use 'cael' in that situation?

Howard: Ah, good, I was coming to that. Well, you would use a future form of 'cael' – 'ga' i' – which conveys 'may I have'. 'Ga' i gawl?' is 'may I have soup?'. The answer is 'Cewch!' – 'You may!', the familiar answer is 'Cei'. So, 'Ga' i gawl?' 'Cewch'. 'Ga' i eistedd 'ma?' 'Cei.' Remember that 'Ga' i' + verb = 'may I have ...?', and 'Ga' i' + noun = 'may I ...?' And also remember that the word after 'ga' i' is soft mutated where appropriate.

Rob: And what if we want to refuse if someone asks us something?

Howard: Well, the negative of 'cewch' is 'na chewch' – 'you may not', and for the familiar form the negative is 'na chei'.

Mike: Hmm. Lot to remember there!

Howard: Yes, there is, so let's have a go. See how you get on with this: cyfieithwch y frawddegau 'ma:

Your turn!

I'm having a good time in Paris.	
I have a cup of tea at 11 o'clock.	
I get petrol in the village.	

The children are not allowed to play on the road.	

Some idioms including 'cael'

cael blas ar rywbeth	to enjoy something	**cael a chael**	touch and go
cael bywyd ci	to have a dog's life	**cael cam**	to be wronged
cael cathod bach	to have kittens/get agitated	**cael dau ben llinyn ynghyd**	to make both ends meet
cael y llaw ucha	to get the upper hand	**cael siom ar yr ochr orau**	to be agreeably surprised
cael hwyl ar	to enjoy	**cael llond bol ar**	to have enough of (lit. to have a belly-full)

(Idioms taken from *Welsh Phrases for Learners,* Leonard Hayles, Y Lolfa, £5.95)

Coffee time

Howard: Now we've had a shot of caffeine, perhaps I can bring up something else to do with 'cael'.

Anka: There's a lot of it, isn't there!

Howard: It's a very versatile verb indeed. I mentioned the passive use of it in the workshop, but I thought we had enough to be getting on with. I try not to introduce too many things in the same session!

Mike:	No, just two would do nicely.
Anka:	We'd never learn Welsh then, Mike!
Marian:	So what's this 'passive' thing, then, Howard?
Howard:	Well, take the riveting sentence, 'John is writing the letter'. In Welsh, we use the construction, 'The letter is having its writing by John'! 'Mae'r llythyr yn cael ei ysgrifennu gan John.' And another: 'Mrs Simpson is opening the college.' What would the English literal construction be?
Sally:	Er … The college is …
Rob:	… having its opening by Mrs Simpson' – ?
Howard:	What teamwork! Well done, you two! And yn Gymraeg?
Dafydd:	Mae'r coleg yn cael ei agor gan Mrs Simpson.
Howard:	Da iawn! I'm not going to labour the point now, because there are other things to take into consideration …
Mike:	Or to have their taking into consideration?
Howard:	Something like that! It's an interesting principle, isn't it.
Marian:	Can I ask you something else? I bought a teatowel yesterday and it says Welsh is the oldest language in Europe. Is this true?
Howard:	How old is any language? Languages change constantly, so it's not that easy to say when Welsh 'started'. However, it can be traced back in a recognisable form to the time when Brythonic was rapidly evolving into what we now call Cymraeg. Dialects of Brythonic were being spoken all over the island of Britain before the Romans arrived here in 55 BC.
Dafydd:	Wasn't it spoken in the north of England? Cumbria and up there?
Howard:	It went up as far as southern Scotland. When the Romans came here, Brythonic absorbed quite a few Latin words. When the Romans left Wales in 383 AD, Brythonic started to evolve into early Welsh. The roots of the other Celtic language, Cornish, Breton, Irish, Scots Gaelic and Manx, are just as old as Welsh.
Marian:	Geraint told me the other day that there are lots of Latin words in Welsh, and I didn't believe him!
Howard:	He's right! And if you've learned any French you'll recognise them too. How about these: bridge: pont in French, Latin and Welsh. Window: fenêtre in French, ffenest in Welsh. Church: église in French, eglwys in Welsh. Book: livre in French, llyfr in Welsh.
Marian:	Oh dear – it's humble pie for tea again, then!

Learner of the Month: Jill Roberts

'I have been learning Welsh since 1998, but when I was a schoolgirl in the 1960s, I had Welsh classes in school, as a second language.

As an adult who is learning Welsh, I have come across some problems:

• I was born and brought up in Aberystwyth, therefore I know a lot of people in the area. A lot of them are first-language Welsh-speakers, but know me as someone who spoke only English. Therefore, this is a problem: they can't change to speak to me in Welsh! I have friends who phone me and start the conversation with, 'Helo, siwmai heddiw, mae'n braf. Sut mae'r dosbarthiadau Cymraeg yn mynd?' – and then they say something like, 'Well, now, here's what I want to talk about', and the conversation changes to English!

• When I started to learn the language, I wasn't confident. When I tried to say something, and I didn't know the Welsh word in a sentence, I lost confidence again. Therefore, it was a big hurdle for me. Now, I carry on and put the English word in the sentence. Don't stop speaking Welsh because one word is lost! Keep at it!

But the advantages of speaking Welsh are endless. For example:

• It opens up a new world – I sing in a Welsh choir and we have competed in the National Eisteddfod. We also sing in plygain services in Montgomeryshire and Penrhyncoch. That is very interesting.

I'm interested in Welsh poetry, and it's a pleasure to understand some of the Welsh songs. I competed on the stage in the Pavilion in the National Eisteddfod in 2004 and 2005. It was a special experience.

• At work, I can deliver a better service having learned Welsh.

• I enjoy S4C and Radio Cymru.

• I've met lots of interesting people through learning Welsh.'

Glossary

cawl	soup	siomedig	disappointing
ffordd	road	siom	disappointment
cath fach	kitten	dosbarth	class
llaw/dwylo	hand/hands	llond bol	enough – slang – lit. belly-full
blas	taste	parcio	to park
llinell/llinellau	line/lines	cael	to have (etc)

Mae Figaro yn cael hwyl yn y cwdyn!

June/ Mehefin

Two months, then, away from the end of the basic Wlpan course, and then time for preparation for the August course. I spoke with a lot of people who had done it in the past and swore it was the best decision they'd ever made. They all told me, though, to keep some time for resting, because it was an exhausting course.

I already knew I was going to miss a day during the first week. I'd joined a small choir of learners, and we were practising for the Canu Gwerin (folk song) class in the Pabell y Dysgwyr (learners' tent) at the Eisteddfod Genedlaethol, which was to be held that year in Meifod, Sir Drefaldwyn (Montgomeryshire). (The Eisteddfod is always the first week in August, and is held alternately in the north and the south of the country.) The first practice I went to was almost my last! The choir coach, Bethan, was a Welsh-speaker, and chattered away in fast Welsh. And only in Welsh! The more advanced learners understood her perfectly – or at least enough to be able to do what she said! I was lost! Fortunately, I found another alto who was prepared to mutter translations in my ear when I asked for them. Thank goodness! And a couple of the singers had a lower level of Welsh than me, which was encouraging – I could tell how far I'd come in the last few months.

It was a delightful experience, rehearsing with the group. Bethan's way of teaching us a song was quite different from anything I'd experienced in choirs in England! More relaxed, more laid-back, but she got what she wanted from us just the same. She was aware that she could teach us to 'Eisteddfod standard', which would mean much more work than we were doing, but she, and we, decided just to go and enjoy taking part. We laughed a lot.

Because there were various communications with the members of the group, I decided that it was time to put a Welsh message onto our answering machine! I decided on a message, wrote it down, and read it carefully on to the machine. It sounded awful – I'd quite obviously read it! No spontaneity at all! So I practised it a few times and then just spoke it. That very evening someone phoned and left a message in Welsh! Fortunately I had asked them to speak 'yn araf ac yn glir' (slowly and clearly), and they did, because I hadn't realised what a challenge it would be to take the message down! Including the phone number, which most people rattle off automatically. I had to play it about six times before I knew for sure who had phoned, and why, and how I could call them back!

The most scary thing that happened that month was that I was asked by a friend to second a motion at an annual Conference. From the stage, in Welsh. I refused. He persisted. I decided to be grown-up and have a go. I had to speak to about a hundred people, for 'just' three minutes ... and speaking Welsh for three minutes sounded far more than I could do in one go!

 ## Book of the month

Six Thousand Welsh Words: a comprehensive basic vocabulary
Ceri Jones (Gomer, £8.95)

The Gwasg Gomer catalogue says this is: 'A comprehensive vocabulary of modern Welsh divided into twenty lists according to subject matter covering the whole spectrum of modern life and including idiomatic, domestic and slang forms.' Just what we need – Welsh is not just a literary language, but a living language, and we learners need to know the slang forms as much as we need the 'correct' stuff!

12 June: Dydd y Dywysoges Gwenllian/ Princess Gwenllian's Day

One of my heroes is Gwenllian. She was the beloved wife of Gruffudd ap Rhys. In 1136, Gruffudd rode off to get help against the Normans. In his absence, the Norman Maurice de Londres decided to get rid of her, knowing her influence in Cymru. She decided to go out as leader of her army, not knowing of the treachery of some of her fellow-countrymen. She and her army were ambushed, one of her beloved sons was killed, and the other injured. Gwenllian was then beheaded in front of her defeated army. She is remembered as one of the bravest Welsh patriots, and there is a memorial stone to her opposite the entrance to Cydweli castle in the south. (Read *Gwenllian: The Welsh Warrior Princess*, by Peter Newton (Gwasg Carreg Gwalch, 2002))

 ## Website of the month

Bwrdd Croeso: www.visitwales.co.uk

A lovely site, lots of beautiful photos, and many ideas for holidays, trips round the country, etc. The more I see of Cymru, the more I realise I don't know, so even if you live here, consider taking your holidays here and discovering more of its beauty and diversity.

The Welsh National Anthem

Mae Hen Wlad Fy Nhadau/Land of my Fathers

We have one of the best anthems in the world! It's incredibly singable and inspiring. It was written in January 1856 by Evan James and his son from the south of Wales. When it was sung at the National Eisteddfod at Bangor in 1874, it was quickly recognised as the song which expressed Welsh national sentiment better than any other.

The anthem is sung on many occasions, not least before a rugby game, and if you learn it, you will feel much more part of the nation. My translation here is deliberately not poetic or 'singable'! – learn it in Welsh, and absorb some of the 'hwyl'!

Mae hen wlad fy nhadau yn annwyl i mi,
Gwlad beirdd a chantorion enwogion o fri;
Ei gwrol ryfelwyr, gwladgarwyr tra mad,
Dros ryddid collasant eu gwaed

The land of my fathers is dear to me,
Land of renowned bards and singers;
Its manly warriors, true patriots,
For freedom spilled their blood.

Chorus:
Gwlad! gwlad! Pleidiol wyf i'm gwlad;
Tra mor yn fur i'r bur hof bau,
O bydded i'r hen iaith barhau.

Land! Land! I support my land;
While the sea is a wall to this fair land,
The old language will survive.

mis 12

Welsh Workshop

Dafydd: Wel! Sesiwn olaf!

Sally: Anodd credu! Ond 'dyn ni'n siarad Cymraeg!

Anka: Diolch am gasglu'r arian i brynu anrheg i Howard. Rw i wedi prynu potel o win coch neis. Mae o'n hoffi gwin coch.

Mike: Gwin drud.

Sally: Wel, 'dyn ni'n ddiolchgar iawn i Howard. Mae e wedi bod yn diwtor ardderchog.

Howard: Helo!

Rob: [Yn sibrwd] Yn gyflym, Anka, cuddia'r gwin dan y bwrdd 'ma! Bore da, Howard!

Howard: Beth sy'n digwydd?

Anka: Dim byd!

Marian: Dim byd o gwbl!

Howard: Hmmm. Wel, mi gawn ni weld am hynny! Rŵan 'ta. Llawer i'w wneud heddiw.

Mike: Gwaith?

Howard: Gwaith, ia, Mike. Dw i eisiau edrych ar y 'past tense' ('the preterite' for techies) eto, gyda 'gwneud', neu 'ddaru' yn y gogledd, ac 'inflected verbs'.

Rob: Wel, even I know what a verb is, but what on earth are 'inflected verbs'?

Howard: They are verbs which have endings which indicate the tense and the person. For example – agor = to open. If you add -ais to the end of it – agorais, 'I opened'. In speech. we include the 'I' bit as well:

Agorais i = I opened. Agorais i'r drws – I opened the door.

If the verb ends in a vowel – such as talu – to pay, prynu – to buy, postio – to post, you chop the last vowel off and this forms what we call the 'stem' – so we get tal-, pryn-, posti-, and to these stems we add the endings.

So, Talais i = I paid.   Prynais i = I bought.   Postiais i = I posted.

In the north, we tend to use the particle 'mi' at the start and soft mutate the verb. We also pronounce this ending as 'es' and also spell it that way rather than '-ais':

Mi dales i = I paid   Mi brynes i = I bought   Mi bosties i = I posted.

In the south, we tend to use the particle 'fe' instead of 'mi', and it also causes the verb to soft mutate:

Fe dales i = I paid   Fe brynes i = I bought   Fe bosties i = I posted

But you'll always find someone somewhere who disagrees with this! -ais is also the ending used in literary Welsh. As far as learners' materials are concerned, some give –es and others give –ais.

Mike: What's the 'mi', then?

Howard: The 'mi' can be used in all persons – its just an indicator which says 'the next bit is a positive statement'. Here are all the endings for the different persons:

-es	I
-est	you (sing/fam)
-odd	he/she/it
-on	we
-och	you (plural)
-on	they

So we have, for example,

Prynodd Idris y llaeth – Idris bought the milk.

Sally: What about, 'Idris bought milk'?

Howard: Then we omit the 'y', and 'llaeth' is soft mutated: 'Prynodd John laeth.'
              So, Anka, what about 'Sioned posted the letter'?

Anka: Oh – I think it's 'Postiodd Sioned y llythyr'.

Howard: Da iawn! And 'Sioned posted a letter'?

Dafydd: 'Postiodd Sioned lythyr'.

Howard: Da iawn! Gwych!

Rob: I'd love to think that all verb stems are so simple, but I'm sure you're going to tell me they're not!

Howard: Quite right! Here are a few others:

Verb	Stem
yfed	yf-
rhedeg	rhed-
gwrando	gwrandaw-
cerdded	cerdd-
eistedd	eistedd (its own stem)

Howard: It's worth knowing how [mynd' – to go – is used. We hear it often.

es i	I went
est ti	you went
aeth e/hi	he/she went
aethon ni	we went
aethoch chi	you went
aethon nhw	they went

For ' dod', we just put a 'd' in front of these – des i = I came. With gwneud, we put 'gwn' in front of these – gwnes i = I did, I made.
But once you've got the correct stem, just add the appropriate ending.
Try these:

Your turn!
They ran.
I walked.
We listened.
She sat.
I drank the milk.
I ate the bread.
I ran a mile.
She ate bread.

Coffee time

Dafydd: I can't believe this is our last workshop. Howard, thanks so much. It's a brilliant idea, and I've really found it helpful. In the classes we have to move fast with learning the language, but here I've found I could talk about the language too, and that's made things much more interesting.

Sally: Last weekend we decided that the whole family would speak nothing but Welsh!

Mike: That was a quiet weekend, then!

Rob: [laughs] No, in fact we talked quite a lot! But what Sally and I found was that, because the children speak better Welsh than we do, we had to listen to them more! It did us all good!

Howard: That's great – your Welsh has improved in leaps and bounds, but it's also proving good for your family relationships! What about the rest of you?

Sally: What do you enjoy doing now in Welsh which you couldn't do before? And what has changed in your attitude to Welsh and being in Wales? The other thing I've found is that if I try to do my shopping in Welsh, as much as I can, well, people were very friendly before, but now when I go into shops in town I get broad smiles. I've never said this before, but I'm beginning to feel I belong. And the funny thing is, I didn't realise, before I spoke Welsh, that I didn't feel I belonged! Perhaps the difference, when I really think about it, is that the Cymry feel I want to belong!

Rob: Yes, I've noticed that. And I've also noticed how much happier Sally is! But our children are having to be careful now – when they whisper in Welsh, I can often understand them – that feels good to me, but they don't like it much!

Mike: I'm beginning to enjoy being able to speak Welsh with people in the pub and at work. I don't quite know what's happened, but there's been some kind of breakthrough. I think I had a mental block at first – not just about Welsh, but about languages in general. Welsh was a handy target.

Howard: Were you good at languages at school?

Mike: No, not at all. A total dunce. I hated it. So I'm amazed I can use Welsh in my social life.

Anka: I was good at languages at school – we had to be, in Slovenia – and I love the breakthroughs and the process of learning a language. Someone asked me last week if I came from Caernarfon!

Howard: Well done, Anka. That's a good feeling, isn't it. What about you, Marian?

Marian: Well, you remember how I said I used to switch off when Geraint's family were chatting in Welsh? I don't now, I can join in, or at least understand the conversation enough to make the right noises in the right places! And Geraint loves it when I whisper things to him in Welsh.

Mike: What things, Marian? Do tell us!

Marian: [laughs] You get your own whisperer!

Mike: Well … Actually … well …

Anka: Oh, go on, Mike!

Mike: Well … er … Anka and I are … well, we're engaged!

All: LLONGYFARCHIADAU!

Learner of the Month: Howard Edwards

You know Howard fairly well by now (but not his dire sense of humour at first hand – be thankful for small mercies!), but here is his story of how he learned Welsh.

'Right, so I've written a few pieces in Jen's book as help and encouragement to those of you who want to go for it and get fluent in Welsh. That was my target when I started off. So why did I want to learn? Well, I was Welsh-born, of Welsh parents and there were and still are Welsh speakers in my extended family. I grew up in Y Fenni and had virtually zero Welsh input there apart from a few odd Welsh words that my mother used to use in English sentences. She would say things like: 'Do you want some more bara menyn?' But I was never able to put even the simplest of Welsh sentences together. As I matured (!) into adulthood, I felt increasingly uncomfortable with claiming myself to be Welsh and not able to speak what I saw as 'my own language'.

'I started my love affair with Welsh language and culture in 1980 with a Linguaphone course, which took me about 18 months to complete. Basil Davies, the Distance tutor, was very encouraging, and I owe him a lot for helping me to get through that course. I did some weekend courses and eventually, in 1984, a summer school in the University of Bangor. This was the turning point. The tutor, Glenys, had a terrific sense of humour and her tutoring was excellent. After that, I enrolled for the University's Welsh grammar course by post. In 1985 I took the old O-Level for adults, and in 1986 I sat the A level, and passed. Between 1987 and 1988 I plodded on under my own steam, reading *Y Cymro* every week and studying novels and bits of poetry – in fact, anything I could get my hands on, including maths and science books in Welsh. I developed an interest in linguistics – the study of human language – and in 1989 I started a three-year BA degree in Welsh and Linguistics at Bangor.

'In the '90s I started, on a very small scale, teaching Welsh to adults. This gradually increased, particularly when I completed my PGCE for Adult and Further Education in 1996. Welsh for Adults was my main subject on this course. Between 1996 and 2000 I worked for Coleg Menai. In December 2000 I took on the post of Head Tutor at the National Centre for Language and Culture, Nant Gwrtheyrn. I'm now working for Popeth Cymraeg in the north

mis
12

of the country.

'When I started learning Welsh, the idea of being a Welsh-language tutor couldn't have been further from my mind. I need to stress here – I was not particularly 'gifted' in languages at school – I found them a real turn-off. But learning Welsh as an adult opened a whole new world for me. If you are thinking of learning Welsh, take the plunge – but beware! It could change your whole life!

'Here's the bottom line. Why did I learn Welsh? Because I really wanted to. There's no better reason, in my opinion.'

Howard yn bwyta 'cod a sglods'.

Glossary

môr	sea	**dysgwr/dysgwyr**	learner/learners
gwasg	press	**collasant**	lost, spilt
tywysog/tywysoges	prince/princess	**gwaed**	blood
hen	old	**pleidiol**	favourable, partial
gwlad	country, nation	**milltir**	mile
tadau	fathers	**anrheg**	present
annwyl	dear	**parhau**	to survive, continue
bardd/beirdd	bard/bards	**cuddio**	to hide
cantorion	singers	**gwneud/ddaru**	to do/did (north Wales)
enwogion	famous men	**postio**	to post
gwrol	brave	**talu**	to pay
rhyfelwyr	warriors	**prynu**	to buy
gwladgarwyr	patriots	**agor**	to open
rhyddid	freedom		

July / *Gorffennaf*

The conference was held in a theatre in Harlech. My nervousness throughout the morning didn't help my enjoyment of the conference one little bit! But eventually the motion was proposed, and I got up to second it. I took a deep breath first, and then set off into the unknown! It must have been painfully obvious to people that I was a) a learner, and b) reading, rather than speaking spontaneously! But they listened, they laughed (in the right places!), and they applauded extraordinarily warmly at the end. I couldn't believe what I'd done. My confidence went up another few notches.

It wasn't the 'doing' of this that boosted my confidence, though. It was their reaction. And that does it for me, every time – the support of the Welsh-speakers and their enthusiasm for someone learning their language. I suppose it's a fault in me – I love to make people happy! And to see that reaction spurs me on to do more.

That was another day spent speaking nothing but Welsh. I didn't always understand people's Welsh – again, lots of different accents and dialects. But they helped me, and what was more, they obviously understood MY Welsh!

On the 15th of July, I had a meal with my 'Challenger' friend. We chatted about all sorts of things – politics, campaigning, books we were reading, travelling, mutual friends, books we were writing. Wide-ranging. And then, as we were walking back to my car, he turned to me, and said, 'Wel, Jen, mae e'n hollol anhygoel, ond wyt ti wedi ennill!' [Well, Jen, it's quite unbelievable, but you've won!']

'Sorry?' I asked, 'won what?'

'We have just had a meal together, and with not a word of English! Didn't you realise? And with six weeks to go before 1 September!'

I was astounded! No, I hadn't realised! I'd spoken Welsh the whole evening, and hadn't realised! Faulty Welsh, sure, but I had proved to myself, and to The

Challenger, that I could communicate in Welsh, which was the idea in the first place. He was delighted. And so was I. And I couldn't believe it either!

So all that hard work had paid off. All the in-at-the-deep-end stuff. All the challenges along the way had added up to beating The Challenge. All the struggles and anxiety had been worthwhile. The initial Challenge was to hold a natural, continuous, fluent conversation, only in Welsh, for several hours, and understand and be understood. I had done it. Even *before* the August four-week course! Ten and a half months since The Challenge was issued. Twelve months exactly since I left the Nant after the summer course. I don't know how I drove home that night. I don't remember it at all! I was as high as a kite. I couldn't stop grinning.

Would I have achieved it without The Challenge? I very much doubt it. I think that without it, all the discouragements and mental blocks would have made me give up by Christmas. That deadline was looming above me, calling me, mocking me, the whole year. Every time I thought about dropping out, I knew I would lose. I think The Challenger knew that The Challenge would drive me on. At times I cursed him! But now I thank him, from the bottom of my heart. On paper, and publicly:

DIOLCH O GALON!

And from that time on …

Well, for a start there was the Eisteddfod at Meifod. And how different it was from the year before, when I'd felt a total outsider. The weather was blazingly hot, which made a change from the disastrous weather at Tyddewi. I was working on an organisation's stand on the first Saturday – the quietest day of the week – and got to know a few people, and used my Welsh, and felt a bit more part of things.

On the Monday I started started on the four-week Wlpan Uwch (higher) course, and I realised it was going to be quite a hard month …

On Thursday morning I drove to the Eisteddfod Maes, and joined the other members of our singing group, Cantorion Aberystwyth. We chatted away in various calibres of Welsh, until it was time for the competition – which, to our astonishment, we won. I spent the rest of the day on the stand, and similarly on the final Saturday. After the exertions of the course throughout the week, and the Eisteddfod, and the incredible hot weather, I was ready to relax on the Sunday!

Then back to the course. We were all a bit nervous because we were going to get Felicity for our tutor that week. Now, Felicity is famous in Ceredigion's Welsh classes, and people are a bit scared of her! I'd heard all sorts of rumours! But within half an hour we were laughing and enjoying ourselves. Felicity is great. She never puts people on the spot. She's an inventive teacher, and again, one who works hard out of the classroom. She rarely speaks English in class, but the amount you learn in an hour with a tutor like that is phenomenal. The Wlpan course carried on throughout August, in blazing heat, and somehow I survived the four weeks.

And then came the Challenge Celebration – and from it came the idea for this book.

That evening, of course, it was time to make further decisions about what I was going to do with my Welsh, and to give myself further targets. I determined to be as near to native-speaker level as possible by Christmas 2004, and to be writing in Welsh by the next Christmas (which, I have to report, I still haven't quite achieved, but I'm getting there). Someone once said to me that written Welsh gets easier the more you read. Obviously true, and that became one of my short-term aims: to read more Welsh books.

I had a long period when talking in Welsh on the phone was really difficult. I couldn't 'do' it without seeing a face, body language, etc. It's so much easier to guess what people mean when you can see them! But it has got easier – even though for a while I needed to ask people to talk a bit slower. I can manage, even though I don't always hear every word someone says. (This can get me into trouble – I am still far too ready to act on what I think I've heard, rather than asking again for clarification.)

For many months, there were still a few people I couldn't have a conversationin Welsh with. I could speak Welsh to them, but I couldn't understand *their* Welsh! However, with time, that has got easier, and I can even talk on the phone in Welsh with them now.

I enjoy watching programmes on S4C – for a long time I always used the subtitles, though. I found it more helpful to listen to the Welsh, know what is being said because of the subtitles, and find phrases and words in the Welsh that I could use elsewhere. I continued to try without the subtitles, but I wasn't quite ready. But I kept trying, and now I can watch programmes without the subtitles – especially things like Pobl y Cwm, where you have the situation, faces, body language and so on to help.

I carried on with my classes too. And guess who the tutor was? The 'terrifying' Felicity! I love her classes. I can't think why she has got this reputation of being frightening! She's great. But she expects people to work hard – could that be the reason she worries people? What I didn't take advantage of – silly me, when it's something I want to work on! – was her offer to mark written work.

So there you have it! That's me. Still working hard on 'the language of the heavens', but feeling much more relaxed about things now. Not driven. (Not driven enough, perhaps!) Needing to do a lot more work on perfecting the language, but able to use it in daily life. Wonderful. Three years on from starting to learn Welsh, I got a job for a while with a company that works in Welsh – another means of developing the language! I passed Safon Uwch – the equivalent, for adult learners, of A-Level Welsh, and I also enrolled on a course on Welsh poetry – that was a bit ambitious, and I was out of my depth, but they were lovely people, and I learned a lot.

What about *you*? What are *your* deadlines? What challenges are you giving *yourself* – a five-year plan, but also daily small challenges? Try it, but you'll need the attitude as well. Let me know how you get on. And remember what I was told when I started. It has echoed in my ears many times since I started learning Welsh:

'When you feel like giving up – keep going!'

Word list

Nouns

amser	time
anrheg	present, gift
ateb	answer, response
bara	bread
bardd	poet
blas	taste
blwyddyn	year
brawd	brother
brecwast	breakfast
bwrdd	table, board
bwyd	food
cân	song
cantorion	singers
car	car
carped	carpet
cath fach	kitten
cawl	soup
chwaer	sister
clinig	clinic
coffi	coffee
criced	cricket
crochenydd	potter
croeso	welcome
cwm	valley
cwpwrdd	cupboard
cwrw	beer
cwmwl	cloud
cynghanedd	form of Welsh poetry
dosbarth	class
dŵr	water
dydd	day
dyn	man
dysgwr	learner
eira	snow
enwogion	famous people
ffenest	window
ffon	stick
ffôn	phone
ffordd	road, way
ffrind	friend
fodca	Vodka
gaeaf	winter
gair	word
garej	garage
garlleg	garlic
gem	gem (stone)
gêm	game
glan	bank of a river
glaw	rain
gorsedd	throne
gwaed	blood
gwallt	hair
gwanwyn	spring (season)
gwasg	press
gwleidyddiaeth	politics
gweithdy	workshop
gwin	wine
gwlad	country, land
gwladgarwyr	patriots
gwraig-tŷ	housewife
gwynt	wind
haf	summer
haul	sun
heddi(w)	today
heno	tonight
hydref	autumn
landin	landing (top of stairs)
linell	line
llaeth/llefrith	milk (s/n)
llaw	hand
llawer	a lot
llên	literature
llond bol	belly-full
llongyfarchiadau	congratulations

164

llyfr	*book*
llyfrgell	*library*
llygad	*eye*
lolfa	*living room*
maes	*field*
merch	*girl*
milltir	*mile*
môr	*sea*
morfa	*sea-marsh*
myfyriwr	*student*
Nadolig	*Christmas*
nant	*stream*
neithiwr	*last night*
newyddion	*news*
niwl	*fog*
nofel	*novel*
pabell	*tent*
pafin	*pavement*
papur	*paper*
papur newydd	*newspaper*
pawb	*everybody*
peint	*pint*
pen	*head*
pen blwydd	*birthday*
penillion	form of Welsh poetry
pensaer	*architect*
plant	*children*
plentyn	*child*
plygain	*cock-crow; Welsh carol service*
pobl	*people*
poced	*pocket*
potel	*bottle*
priodas	*marriage*
rhew	*frost*
rhyfelwyr	*warrior*
roced	*rocket*
seidr	*cider*
sesiwn	*session*
sglodion	*chips*
sgwrs	*conversation, talk*
siec	*cheque*
siocled	*chocolate*
sioe	*show*
siom	*disappointment*
Sir	*county*
swper	*supper*
syniad	*idea*
tad(au)	*father(s)*
tafarn	*pub*
talwrn y beirdd	a competition between poets
tatws	*potatoes*
tebot	*teapot*
teledu	*television*
tiwtor	*tutor*
to bach	*small roof/circumflex accent*
tonig	*tonic*
tŷ	*house*
tywsog(es)	*prince/ess*
unrhywun	*anyone*
ysgol	*school (or ladder!)*

Verbs

adnabod/nabod	*to know (people, places)*
agor	*to open*
astudio	*to study*
bwrw glaw	*to rain*
bwyta	*to eat*
byw	*to live*
cael	*to have*
canmol	*to praise*
canu	*to sing*
carlam	*to gallop*
caru	*to love*
chwarae	*to play*
cicio	*to kick*
cnocio	*to knock*

coginio	to cook
colli	to lose
cuddio	to hide
cusanu	to kiss
cwrdd	to meet
cymharu	to compare
cytuno	to agree
darllen	to read
deall	to understand
dechrau	to start
dod	to come
dysgu	to learn
eistedd	to sit
gweithio	to work
gweld	to see
gwneud	to do/to make
gwybod	to know (things)
hoffi	to like
malu	to grind/to mince/to smash
meddwl	to think
mwynhau	to enjoy
mynd	to go
neidio	to jump
parcio	to park
parhau	to survive/to continue
plannu	to plant
postio	to post
priodi	to marry
prynu	to buy
pysgota	to fish
talu	to pay
yfed	to drink
ymddeol	to retire
ymlacio	to relax
ysgrifennu	to read

Adjectives – Ansoddeiriau

ail	second
anhygoel	unbelievable
annwyl	dear
anodd	difficult
arall	other
ardderchog	excellent
bach	small
braf	fine, good
byr	short
canolig	medium
cenedlaethol	national
coch	red
cryf	strong
cyffrous	exciting
cyflym	fast
cymylog	cloudy
da	good
ddrwg	bad
denau	thin
diflas	miserable, boring
distaw	silent
drud	expensive
du	black
glân	clean
gorau	best
gwael	vile
gwell	better
gwlyb	wet
gwrol	brave
gwyn	white
gwyntog	windy
gwyrdd	green
hapus	happy
hen	old
heulog	sunny
hwyr	late
ifanc	young
llawen	merry

lwcus	*lucky*
mawr	*big*
melyn	*yellow*
melys	*sweet*
mwy	*more*
neis	*nice*
nesa(f)	*next*
newydd	*new*
niwlog	*foggy*
oer	*cold*
ofnadw(y)	*awful*
pleidiol	*partial*
poeth	*hot*
rhewllyd	*frosty*
siomedig	*disappointing*
Slofenaidd	*Slovenian*
stormus	*stormy*
sych	*dry*
tal	*tall*
tawel	*quiet*
ymlaciol	*relaxing*

Adverbs

yn amlwg	*obviously*
yn anffodus	*unfortunately*
yn araf	*slowly*
yn dawel	*quietly*
yn ddistaw	*silently*
yn enwedig	*especially*
yn gyflym	*quickly*
yn hollol	*absolutely*
yn swnllyd	*noisily*
yn wreiddiol	*originally*

Prepositions

allan	*out*
dros	*over*
i	*to*
o	*from*
yn	*in*

Names

Yr Alban	*Scotland*
Calennig	*New Year's presents*
Cei Bach	*Little Quay*
Cymru	*Wales*
Cymry Cymraeg	*Welsh-speaking*
	Welsh people
Gwrtheyrn	*Vortigern*
Yr Hen Galan	*The old new year*
Morgannwg	*Glamorgan*
S4C	*Sianel Pedwar*
	Cymru
Ynys Enlli	*Bardsey Island*

Other

blwyddyn newydd dda!	*Happy New Year!*
bore da	*good morning*
bore 'ma	*this morning*
da iawn	*very good*
nos da	*good night*
os gweli di'n dda	*please (familiar)*
os gwelwch yn dda	*please (formal/ plural)*
tan	*until*
wrth gwrs	*of course*
y	*the*
y bore (y.b.)	*a.m.*

Welsh in a Year is just one of a whole range of publications for Welsh-language learners from Y Lolfa. For a full list of books currently in print, send now for your free copy of our new, full colour catalogue. Or simply surf into our website

www.ylolfa.com

for secure on-line ordering.

TALYBONT CEREDIGION CYMRU SY24 5AP
e-bost ylolfa@ylolfa.com
gwefan www.ylolfa.com
ffôn (01970) 832 304
ffacs 832 782